The Torn Veil

The Torn Veil

The Story of Sister Gulshan Esther
as told to
Thelma Sangster
with Noble Din interpreter

C.L.C. BOOKS
Fort Washington, Pennsylvania 19034

C.L.C. BOOKS
Box 1449, Fort Washington, PA 19034

Copyright © 1984
Sister Gulshan Esther and Thelma Sangster

First published in 1984 by
Marshall, Morgan and Scott Publications, Ltd.

First American edition 1989
under special arrangements with the
British publisher.
This printing 1995

Extracts from *The Koran,* trans. N.J. Dawood
(Penguin Classics, Fourth revised edition 1974)
pp.15, 176-177, 408, 412. Copyrighted © N.J.
Dawood, 1956, 1959, 1966, 1968, 1974. Reprinted
by permission of Penguin Books Ltd.

ISBN 0-87508-473-7

IMPRESO EN COLOMBIA
BUENA SEMILLA
Apartado 29724
Bogotá, Colombia

Printed in Colombia

Contents

'Oh Eagle, don't be despondent
due to the swift and rough breeze,
For it only blows in this manner
to make you fly faster and higher.'

Iqbal

1: To Mecca

I would not in the ordinary course of events have wanted to come to England, that Spring of 1966. I, Gulshan Fatima, the youngest daughter of a Muslim Sayed family, descended from the prophet Mohammed through that other Fatima, his daughter, had always lived a quietly secluded life at home in the Punjab, Pakistan. Not only was this because I was brought up in *pardah* from the age of seven, according to the strict, orthodox Islamic code of the Shias, but also because I was a cripple, and unable even to leave my room without help. My face was veiled from men, other than permitted kinsfolk, like my father and two older brothers, and uncle. For the most part, during those first fourteen years of my feeble existence, the perimeter walls of our large garden in Jhang, about 250 miles from Lahore, were my boundaries.

It was Father who brought me to England – he who looked down on the English for worshipping three gods, instead of One God. He would not even let me learn the infidel language in my lessons with Razia, my teacher, for fear I should somehow become contaminated with error and drawn away from our faith. Yet he brought me, after spending large sums in a fruitless search for treatment at home, to seek the best medical advice. He did this out of kindness and concern for my future happiness, but how little we knew as we landed at Heathrow airport that early April day, of the trouble and sadness that waited round the corner for our family. Strange that I, the crippled child, the weakest of his five children, should have become in the end the strongest of all, and a rock to shatter all he held dear.

I have only to shut my eyes, even now in maturity, and a picture rises before me of my father, dear Aba-Jan, so tall and lean in his well-tailored, high-necked black coat trimmed with the gold buttons, over the loose trousers, and on his head the white turban lined with blue silk. I see him, as so often in childhood, coming into my room to teach me my religion.

I see him standing by my bed, opposite the picture of the House of God at Mecca, Islam's holiest place, the *Ka'aba*, erected it is said by Abraham and repaired by Mohammed. Father takes down the Holy Quran from its high shelf, the highest place in the room, for nothing must be put on or above the Quran. He first of all kisses the green silk cover and recites the *Bismillah i-Rahman-ir-Raheem*. (I begin this in the name of God, the Compassionate, the Merciful). Then he unwraps the green silk cover – he has first carefully performed *Wudu*, the ritual ablutions necessary before carrying or touching the holy book. He repeats the *Bismillah* and then places the Holy Quran on a *rail*, a special x-shaped stand, touching the book only with his finger tips. He sits so that I, propped on a chair, can also see. I too have performed *Wudu*, with the help of my maids.

With his finger Father traces the sacred writings in the decorative Arabic script, and I, anxious to please, repeat after him the *Fatiha*, the Opening, words which bind together all Muslims, everywhere:

'Praise be to Allah, Lord of the Creation,
The Compassionate, the Merciful,
King of Judgement-day!
You alone we worship, and to You alone
    we pray for help.
Guide us to the straight path
The path of those whom You have favoured,
Not of those who have incurred Your wrath,
Nor of those who have gone astray.

Today we are reading from the Sura *The Imrans*:

"Allah! There is no God but Him, the Living, the Ever-existent One.

"He has revealed to you the Book with the truth, confirming the scriptures which preceded it: for He has already revealed the Torah and the Gospel for the guidance of men and the distinction between right and wrong."

I am doing what every Muslim child brought up in an orthodox family does from early childhood – reading through the Holy Quran in Arabic. It can only really be understood in the Arabic in which it was written. We Muslims know that it cannot be translated, as if it were just any book, without losing some of its meaning, because it is sacred.

When I shall have finished reading it through for the first time – around the age of seven, regarded as the age of discretion – there will be a feast to celebrate – we call it the 'ameen of the Holy Quran' – and members of the family, friends and neighbours will be invited. In the central open courtyard of our bungalow, where the men sit separated from the women by a partition, the *mullah* will recite prayers to mark my arrival at this important new stage of life, and the women, sitting in their part of the courtyard, will hush their gossip to listen.

We have reached the end of the Sura. Now comes my catechism. Father looks at me with a smile hovering about his lips:

'Well done little *Beiti* (daughter),' he says. 'Now answer me these questions:

'Where is Allah?'

Shyly I repeat the lesson I know so well: 'Allah is everywhere.'

'Does Allah know all the actions you do on earth?'

'Yes, Allah knows all the actions I do on earth, both good and bad. He even knows my secret thoughts.'

9

'What has Allah done for you?'

'Allah has created me and all the world. He loves and cherishes me. He will reward me in heaven for all my good actions and punish me in hell for all my evil deeds.'

'How can you win the love of Allah?'

'I can win the love of Allah by complete submision to His will and obedience to His commands.'

'How can you know the Will and Commands of Allah?'

'I can know the Will and Commands of Allah from the Holy Quran and from the Traditions of our Prophet Mohammed (May peace' and blessings of Allah be upon him).'

'Very good,' says Father. 'Now is there anything you want to know. Have you any questions?'

'Yes, Father, please tell me, why is Islam better than other religions?' I ask him this not because I know anything about other religions but because I like to hear him explain our religion. Father's answer is clear and definite:

'Gulshan, I want you always to remember this. Our religion is greater than any other because, first of all, the glory of God is Mohammed. There were many other prophets, but Mohammed brought God's final message to mankind, and there is no need of any prophet after him. Second, Mohammed is God's Friend. He destroyed all the idols and converted all the people who worshipped the idols to Islam. Third, God gave the Quran to Mohammed, after all the other holy books. It is God's last word and we must obey it. All other writings are incomplete.'

I listen. His words are writing themselves on the tablets of my mind and my heart.

If there is time I ask him to tell me again about the picture in my room. What is it like to go on pilgrimage to the holy city of Mecca, that magnet towards which every Muslim turns to pray five times daily? We turn too in our city, as the *muezzin* calls the *azzan* from the minaret of the mosque. The sound ricochets along the avenues, above the noise of traffic and of the bazaar, and enters our

10

screened windows at dawn, noon, dusk and at night, calling the faithful to prayer with the first declaration of Islam:

"La ilaha ill Allah,
Muhammad rasoolullah!"

"There is no God but Allah:
And Mohammed is the Prophet of Allah."

Father explains it all to me. He has been twice on pilgrimage – once by himself and once with his wife, my mother. It is every Muslim's duty to go at least once in his life – oftener if he is rich enough. To go on pilgrimage is the fifth of the basic Five Pillars of Islam, which unite millions of Muslims in many different countries and ensure the continuance of our faith.

'Will I go to Mecca, Father?' I ask. He laughs and stoops to kiss my forehead.

'You will, little Gulshan. When you are older and perhaps. . . .'

He does not finish the sentence, but I know what he wants to say . . . 'When our prayers for you are answered.'

From these instruction periods I learn devotion to God, an attachment to my religion and its customs, fierce pride in my ancestral line from the Prophet Mohammed, through his son-in-law Ali, and an understanding of the dignity of my father, who is not only the head of our family but, as a descendant of the Prophet, is a *Sayed* and a *Shah*. He is also a *Pir* – religious leader, and a landlord with a large estate in the country and a commodious bungalow surrounded by gardens on the edge of our city. I begin to understand why we are so respected as a family, even by the *mullah*, or *maulvi*, who comes to ask questions of my father, religious questions, which he himself cannot answer.

Looking back now I can trace a purpose in those captive years, when mind and spirit unfolded like the rosebuds in our well-watered garden, tended so lovingly by our gardeners. My name, Gulshan, means in Urdu, 'the place of flowers, the garden.' I, a sickly plant to bear such a name, was tended in the same way by my father. He loved all of us – his two sons Safdar Shah and Alim Shah, and three daughters, Anis Bibi, Samina and me, but although I disappointed him in being born a female, and then when I was six months old, being left a weak cripple by typhoid, Father loved me as much, if not more than the others. Had not my mother given him a sacred charge on her death bed to look after me?

'I beg you Shah-ji, do not marry again, for the sake of little Gulshan,' she said with her dying breath. She wanted to protect me, since a step-mother and her children could reduce the patrimony of a first wife's daughter, and could treat her unkindly if she were ailing and unmarried.

He had promised her those many years ago and he had kept his word, in a land where a man might have up to four wives, according to the Quran, if he were rich enough to treat each one with equality and justice.

Such was the undisturbed pattern of my life, until that visit to England when I was 14. It changed everything in subtle ways, setting in motion a chain of unintended consequences. I had no premonition of this of course as I waited in a London hotel room, on the third day of our visit, with Salima and Sema my maids. We waited for the verdict of the English specialist my father had heard of during the search for treatment in Pakistan, who would settle, once and for all, my future.

If I could be cured of this sickness which had paralysed my left side when I was an infant, then I should be free to marry my cousin, to whom I had been betrothed at three months, and who was now at home in Multan, Punjab, awaiting news of my recovery. And if not, my engagement would have to be broken, and my shame would be greater than if I had been married and then divorced by my husband.

We heard the footsteps coming. Salima and Sema jumped up and arranged their long, scarf-like *dupattas* nervously. Salima pulled mine right down over my face, as I lay on the coverlet of my bed. I was shivering, but not from cold. I had to grit my teeth to stop them from chattering.

The door opened and in walked my father with the doctor.

'Good morning,' said a pleasant, very polite voice. I could not see the face of this Dr David, but he carried with him an air of authority and knowledge. Firm hands pushed up my long sleeve and tested a limp left arm and then my wasted leg. One minute passed and then the specialist straightened up.

'There is no medicine for this – only prayer,' said Dr David to my father. There was no mistaking the quiet finality in his voice.

Lying listening on my couch I heard the name of God used by the strange English doctor. I was puzzled. What could he know of God? I sensed from his kind and sympathetic manner that he was dashing our hopes of my recovery, and yet he had pointed to the way of prayer.

My father walked to the door with him. When he came back he said, 'That was good for an Englishman, telling us to pray.'

Salima turned back my *dupatta* and helped me to sit up.

'Father, can't he make me better?' I could not keep my voice from trembling. Tears were gathering behind my eyes.

Father patted my lifeless hand. He said quickly: 'There's only one way now. Let us knock on the heavenly door. We will go on to Mecca as we intended. God will hear our prayers, and we may yet return home with thanksgiving.'

He smiled at me, and I tried to smile back. My sorrow was equally his sorrow, but he wasn't in despair. There was renewed hope in his voice. Surely at the house of God or at the healing spring of Zamzam we would find our hearts' desire.

We stayed at the hotel for a few more days, while Father arranged for the flight through to Jeddah, the airport used

13

by pilgrims to Mecca. He hadn't done so before, since he was awaiting the outcome of any treatment which might be recommended. He had planned this visit to fall just before the annual month of pilgrimage, so that after treatment we should be able to go to Mecca to give thanks.

During those days of waiting father went out to see friends in the Pakistani community or they came to see him. Ordinarily the women of those families would have visited me. But I felt the shame of my condition and was not accustomed to meeting strangers at home, so few of the ladies knocked at my door. Who would want to see withered limbs, with the skin turned black, wrinkled and hanging loose, and with whatever fingers there were sticking together with all the muscular strength of a piece of jelly? At an age when my peers were beginning to dream of the day when they would wear the red wedding dress, with the gold embroidery, and go jewelled, with a fine dowry to their husband's home, I was facing a lonely future, cut off from my own kind, a non-person, never to be a whole, proper woman, behind a veil of shame.

We were on the second floor of the hotel, in a comfortable room next door to Father's. It had thick carpets and its own bathroom. Apart from tending me, and washing our undies in the bathroom by hand, Salima and Sema, who slept in my room on a folding bed, sitting up in shifts to protect me and see to my needs, had little to do. But time passed quickly enough with my books, the five prayer times and with the ordinary details of washing, dressing, eating, which always take longer when a person is disabled. At other times I listened to the entertaining gossip of my maids. They made occasional forays to the lobby downstairs, but were too frightened to go out alone. Most of the time they contented themselves with a view of the world outside the window, reporting to me what they saw. Their reactions were those of typical village girls of Pakistan, and they made me laugh:

'Oh see the beautiful city' (This from Salima). 'So many people are walking up and down and there are so many cars.'

Then there would be a cry from Sema.

'Oh the women have bare legs. Aren't they ashamed? The men and women are walking together, holding hands. They're kissing. Oh they're going straight to hell.'

We had been taught strict rules about dress and behaviour from our childhood up. We covered ourselves modestly from neck to ankles with the *shalwar kameeze* of the Punjab – a loose tunic and trousers, gathered around the ankle. We wore round our necks a long fine, wide scarf or *dupatta*, which could cover our heads when necessary or be pulled right over our faces, and we also, when it was cold, wrapped ourselves in a shawl. If we had to go out then we wore the *burka* – a long impenetrable veil, covering us from head to toe, gathered into a headpiece, with a net-covered slit in front to see through. It rendered impossible any ordinary conversation in the street, and cut down the wearer's ability to see and hear traffic. But at the time I am speaking of we never questioned the rules that governed our lives, and would indeed have been terrified to defy the conventions. In fact, we felt the veil a protection. We could look out (just) at the world, but it could not look at us.

When we saw how women in London flaunted themselves in their immodest mini-skirts, ending well above the knee, it was obvious to all three of us that it was the wickedest city in the world.

In our country, and even more in our city, to talk to a man who was not of our immediate family, even to male servants, would have brought us into disrepute. The whole purpose of *pardah* was, of course, the protection of family honour. Not the slightest whiff or stain of suspicion must attach itself to the daughters of a Muslim family. The penalties for indiscretion could be terrible.

Three times a day food arrived, brought by a waiter with a trolley. The maids would take it from him at the door. Sometimes it would be accompanied by an English maid, and I would shut my eyes so as not to see her legs.

I was becoming very tired of the hotel food. Father ordered chicken for us every day, as that was *halal*, permitted flesh, slaughtered in the approved manner. Pork

15

was *haram*, forbidden – even to say the name 'pig' made one's mouth dirty, and even to this day I use the Punjabi word *'barla,'* which means 'outsider,' when talking about it, such is the force of early training. Any other kind of meat could also be suspected of having been cooked in lard. With the chicken came vegetables and rice, and ice cream for sweet. We drank Coca Cola, and had a supply of that in our room. I wished vainly for curry or kebabs, and for peaches or mangoes from our trees at home.

Father helped to keep up my spirits by taking me on two or three short outings. Once I was shown around the hotel, and a couple of times he took me, with the servants, for a ride around the neighbourhood in a taxi. He explained to me why the *Ingrez* were not like us:

'This is a Christian country,' he said. 'They believe in Jesus Christ as the Son of God. Of course they are wrong, because God never married and how could He have a Son? Still they are the people of a Book just as we are. Muslim and Christian share the same Book.'

This puzzled me. How could they share our Book and yet be so different?

'They have freedom to do many things that we do not,' he said. 'They have the freedom to eat pork and drink stimulants. There is no distance between men and women. They live together without marrying, and when children grow up they do not respect their elders. But they are good people, very punctual and they have good principles. When they make a promise they keep it. Not like Asians.'

Father was an authority on this subject. He dealt with foreigners all the time in the exporting of the cotton he grew in Pakistan.

'We may differ in religion from them, but they are sympathetic people who will do things for you and they're humane,' he concluded.

I pondered the contradictions of the *Ingrez* – a kind people, living in a gentle, green country, fed by frequent rains, whose Book led to such freedom. Yet our Book was related to theirs. What was the key to this difference between us? It was too deep for a girl of 14 – I dismissed the question from my mind, and gave myself up to anticipation of the Pilgrimage upon which we were embarking. It was many years before further enlightenment came, and when it did I would not be able to dismiss the question so lightly.

2: The Hajj

The beautiful white plane of the Pakistan International Airways sat like a bird on the airstrip. As I was lifted up the gangway, from my wheelchair, I felt a sense of liberation at leaving England. This visit had achieved something, in ending our uncertainty. Now there was only one hope and we were being drawn towards it at great speed. Bathed in diamond-clear light it lay in my dreams, a place unknown to me and yet well known – the holy city of Mecca, which every Muslim desires to see at least once in his or her life.

On the plane we had seats in the first-class compartment, and once again I sat between my maids, with Sema acting as support for my weak left side, and Salima ready to fetch and carry. Father spread himself over two seats in front from where he continued my education in travel:

'We're now flying at 30,000 feet up in the air,' he said, when the plane stopped climbing.

I looked out of the window and gasped. We were in a brilliant world of sunshine and below us was a floor of softest billowy cotton clouds, like the stuffing for a bride's mattress.

Salima and Sema looked out too – and gave muffled little screams:

'Look how much iron is flying through the air,' they marvelled in a mixture of Punjabi and Urdu words, overlaid with their heavy Jhang accent. I suppressed a smile – they were village girls to whom a great deal was happening.

Suddenly the plane began to bounce up and down in the air, and I was frightened. Father explained that we had hit an air pocket: 'Don't worry. Everything is quite safe,' he assured us.

18

There were other pilgrims on the plane. I knew that like us they had in their luggage the white *Ihram* garments, which each pilgrim must wear for *Hajj*, the Pilgrimage.

Once, Father had taken me to see a film about the *Hajj*. It was for religious people, who intended to go to Mecca during the month of Pilgrimage, and it showed all the customs in beautiful colour. I had been taught the history of the birth of our religion in the deserts of Arabia. The landscape of these events was as familiar to me as the dear landscape of our own house and garden.

The stewardess, who was dressed in green, with a token *dupatta* under her chin, brought a meal but I only picked at it. Salima looked at the barely touched food and she said softly:

'Bibi-ji, won't you eat to keep up your strength?'

I shook my head. 'I'm not hungry.' In fact I was feeling rather sick, partly from the bumping of the aircraft and partly from excitement at what lay ahead. I said nothing about my real feelings to her. How could I discuss with a servant the hopes and fears that flitted across my mind like the clouds chasing across the sky?

At Abu Dhabi we changed planes and were joined by pilgrims from far-away places. I studied their costumes with interest, trying to discover where they came from. My teacher Razia had done well. I was able to identify people from Iran, Nigeria, China, Indonesia, Egypt . . . all the world seemed to be moving towards the city of Mecca.

There was a crackling on the loudspeaker. In two languages, English and Arabic, the hostess was telling us that we were approaching Jeddah and preparing to land.

A sign lit up. 'We must fasten our seat belts,' said Father. We did. Salima helped me and Father checked to see that it was properly done.

Out of the plane window I could see the desert, its dun-coloured dunes blown into crescent shapes by the harsh, hot winds; I could see mountains on the horizon, many miles away, and then a large city spread out below us, with tall buildings, and many streets. I could see trees and green gardens.

'See,' said Father, 'What water does to the desert. It is only a few years since they brought the piped water from the Wadi Fatima.'

I nodded. In my lessons I'd learned how oil riches had brought many improvements to a people who had once been poor and backward, living in mud houses, if they were farmers, or bedouin tents, if they were nomads, all going without rain for years at a time.

The plane touched down and there to meet us at the airport was my father's old friend, the Sheikh, with his big Chevrolet car. This Sheikh had eight wives and eighteen children living at his huge villa. Thirteen of his children were daughters and five were young sons. I believe he had others who were married or studying abroad. He had his own oil well, which supported them all in luxury. In addition he was a landowner, breeding cattle and camels, sheep and goats.

I had opportunity to see the workings of this large household, during the next few days, while we enjoyed the Sheikh's hospitality.

The Sheikh introduced me to all of his wives – Fatima, Zora, Rabia, Rukia . . . right down the line.

'I have no favourites,' he announced. 'All my wives are equal.' I knew why he said this – because the Quran makes it plain that a man may marry more than one wife but he must treat all his wives equally well. The Prophet, of course, had several wives, but ordinary men, I was told, found it almost impossible to carry out his instruction about equality with impartiality. Polygamy was not therefore encouraged in our society – yet here it appeared to flourish, and everyone seemed on good terms with each other.

The daughters of the household, the oldest of whom I took to be about 18, were introduced to me by a lady translator, Bilquis. They drifted into the female guest room, where I was established with my maids, to ask me about Pakistan.

'Do you have roads? Cities? What do you eat? What kind of vegetables do you grow? Do you have schools for girls? Do you wear that kind of dress all the time?'

I answered as best I could, and was pleased when they said they wished to go to Pakistan to see it all. I, in turn, asked about their lives: 'How do you live here? What do you do all day?'

The answer seemed to be 'very little.' The Sheikh kept his wives and daughters at home. The daughters, who were well educated, seemed to do little but amuse themselves. They spent their days gossiping, watching TV and doing a little light reading in English and Arabic. Yet they seemed happy enough, with every wish met. If they wanted to go shopping Bilquis went with them and handled the money while they chose whatever they wanted.

As for the Sheikh's wives, apart from shopping trips (in shifts) or visits to the hospital with Bilquis, when they wrapped themselves in black *burkas*, either the full length or the Turkish kind, divided at the waist, their main object seemed to be to please the Sheikh. They sat about cross-legged on cushions wearing gold and silver embroidered kaftans. There were sofas around the walls in the huge marble-floored room but they preferred the floor. Sometimes they dressed Western-style in elaborate and fashionable dresses ordered from England and America, putting on expensive jewellery. The air was heavy with perfume, sprayed by servants.

In the evening, before bed, I was able to meet Father for a few minutes in the public room, to talk, and compare notes.

The Sheikh was 65, according to Father, but his smooth unwrinkled skin hid the years. He was a blend of old ways and new – he especially liked a social life and the company of other men, entertaining them at home both lavishly and generously. He enjoyed smoking and drinking black tea and listening to Arab music, which he had piped into every room, so that all could share his pleasure. This, I learned, was typically Arabic. All the facilities of the house must be shared with everyone, whether wanted or not. I, as it happened, did not understand Arabic music.

Meal times were interesting occasions, when a whole lamb was cooked and served to the household, divided between the men's dining room and the women's. The diners took off their shoes before treading on the colourful Persian carpets. They ate reclining on the thick cushions placed around a circle. A huge tray of spiced rice and steaming lamb was placed in the middle, and around it lay dishes of eggplant, rice, salad, flat sheets of bread and custards or *halva*. Everyone ate with their right hands only, rolling handfuls of rice into lumps and popping them in their mouths, and tearing off pieces of bread.

I ate in my room. I could not balance on those cushions to eat under so many curious eyes. But the Sheikh was kindness itself, allowing me to do as I pleased. My room was full of comforts, such as a beautiful carpet, some green plants, a pretty, shaded round window, a big mirror and a bathroom alcove, with a modern flush toilet.

Hospitality is taken very seriously by the Arabs. It stems from tribal memories of the struggle to survive in the harsh desert, when one's life could depend on being given shelter by the bedouin. It used to be said that, in the old days, a desert sheikh would welcome a guest and entertain him for three days before asking even his name or his business. This sheikh maintained tradition by making available to us all the facilities of his house, including a car and driver while we stayed with him. It meant that we were able to see something of the beautiful city of Jeddah.

Father sat in the front with the white-robed driver, Qazi, while I peered through the curtained rear windows at the city. It was crowded with pilgrims, who poured off the ships in the harbour or who came with every flight into the new airport. Qazi, the driver, pointed out for us many contrasts between old and new – the ten-storey office building along King 'Abd al-'Aziz Street where laden donkeys jostled the big American cars. We saw the *suq*, the street market, where one could buy everything from coffee beans to carpets – even holy water brought down from Mecca – and the shops selling Western merchandise. We saw the old city, with the magnificent, crumbling, tall stone merchants houses, adorned with latticed balconies, from which the women of the *harem* used to peer down at the street life, unseen by those below. In great contrast was the new low-cost housing built on the outskirts of the city.

'When there was no oil there was poverty and other problems,' volunteered Qazi, 'But now we have oil we have good food and the children can learn.'

We stopped to see the oil being pumped out of the ground in one place. I did not like the smell of that.

When we left the Sheikh to travel to Mecca we did so in comfort and style, as he insisted that we take his car and driver. Father thanked him with a little speech:

'You have shown us very warm generosity and friend-ship, to make our journey easy.'

The Sheikh would have done this for any visitor, but I knew that he did it especially for us, because he was an old family friend and business acquaintance of my father's, with an interest in the purchase of the good breed of sheep and goats for which our area was famous.

We left very early in the morning, after prayers, for the drive to Mecca because we wanted to take time and see everything on the way. The new four-lane highway was very good, and fleets of taxis, trucks and buses rushed along, carrying an endless stream of pilgrims forward on the forty-five mile journey to Mecca. There were many on foot, stoically marching forward, prepared to endure what would become a baking plain when the sun rose higher. They did this, not because they were poor, but because they were recalling the journey of Abraham, when he sought for sanctuary for Hagar and Ishmael.

I wouldn't admit it, but I was almost glad to be crippled, so that I did not have to walk under the broiling sun in a caul-dron of heat. I knew this was not the spirit of *Hajj*, which is one of total sacrifice and submission, so I said nothing.

Qazi, the driver, pointed out the water taps along the way, and the electric lights strung on poles which lit the travellers:

'The King has done this. He comes himself with his ministers and the princes and opens the pilgrimage each year, and he has made many improvements to the facilities at the holy places.'

Fifteen miles from the city signs warned us 'Restricted area. Muslims only permitted.' Some of the soldiers at the entry points had guns, and they were examining people's passes. The driver spoke to the soldiers and we were allowed to take the car on.

We made progress very slowly, climbing the hills, through a road cut into the rocks, past a mass of white-robed worshippers who were following the steps of Abraham after Sarah banished the serving-woman and her son.

Our ears were filled with the sound of chanted prayers, verses of the Holy Quran, and the declaration:

'There is no God but Allah. Mohammed is the Prophet of Allah.'

Then we rounded a hill and the holy city, white and shining in the already baking morning sunshine, burst into view below us. The driver stopped the car and the pilgrim's cry broke from our lips in a quite involuntary manner:

'Labbayka Allahumma Labbayka!' 'Here I am, at Thy service. O Allah! Here I am at Thy service; Here I am at Thy service; There is no partner unto Thee; Here I am at Thy service; to Thee the glory, the riches and the sovereignty of the world. There is no partner to Thee.'

'Mohammed's city,' said Father. 'Just think, the Prophet preached in these streets.'

A strange feeling of calm settled on me. All worry about the future lifted. I felt at one with all these other pilgrims, seeking a power I could not see, as eternal and mysterious as the seven hills surrounding the city.

24

3: The water of life

The Hajji-Camp, or pilgrims' rest, was some way from the Haram Mosque. Abdullah, the guide, who had been found for us by our friend, the Sheikh, welcomed us at the entrance. He and Father shook hands and embraced.

'*Alhan Wa salan* (Welcome),' said Abdullah.

'And to you,' said Father, with that easy acceptance of this Arab as a brother and equal, which was such a feature of *Hajj*.

'Please enter. You're welcome in the Name of Allah,' said Abdullah. 'I have received his excellency the Sheikh's letter. I've arranged the rooms for you. . . .' There followed a discussion about lambs for the sacrifice. Father was ordering two for each person, even the maids; that was eight lambs.

A little shiver of delight ran through me. The Feast of Sacrifice *(Eid al Adha)* in honour of the Patriarch Abraham's willingness to sacrifice his son Ishmael, was the high point of the Pilgrimage. Father was making sure our prayers had special efficacy, with the blood of so many lambs.

Our rooms were all in lines, on one level. We had two rooms with bathrooms attached, very simply and plainly furnished, with *charpais* to sleep on. I thought with longing of my cotton-filled mattress on the *palang* at home. Latticed string with a hair mattress on top was not quite so restful, particularly as a paralysed left side made turning over difficult. This, however, was all part of going on Pilgrimage. For days on end hundreds of thousands of people would be packed into the area of Mecca, squashing into the hotels and guest houses, camping in the open air. There would be little comfort about it, and no ostentatious

25

display of wealth. The good would be lost if one voiced complaints, were arrogant and proud, or lost one's temper in the heat and the stressful conditions, so Father explained.

An electric fan in the ceiling of our room moved the hot, thick air around, in a fruitless search for coolness. There were greenish curtains at the window, drawn to keep out the sun, which gave a slight feeling of being in a tank of fishes. In addition there were thin metal screens, through which I could see the distant outlines of the minarets of the Great Mosque, pointing upwards like fingers.

Resting on my *charpai*, I heard the endless shuffling of the heelless leather sandals worn by the pilgrims. Their voices reached us in a babel of strange languages. Weaving through the texture of sound was the hypnotic chanting of verses from the Quran, and *Allahu Akbar* –'God is Most Great.' Excitement prickled through me. To be here was good, enough to live on for a lifetime. My maids felt that too.

'How lucky we are to be your servants, and to be on *Hajj*,' said Salima as she and Sema helped me take my second cool shower of the day. For them it was specially fortunate as many devout persons all over the world were at this moment longing to be here, but could not afford the time or outlay of money. The *Hajj* could take up to one month, if one visited all the holy places.

Father found some of his merchant friends from Lahore, Rawalpindi, Peshawar and Karachi, but for once they were not all talking about the price of cotton and wheat. Oh no, here worldly matters dropped away and also all distinction of birth, national origin, achievements, work or status. In the huge eating-hall at the Hajji-Camp servants sat down to eat with their masters, all differences covered by the *Ihram* – the pilgrim's dress. The men wore a simple unsewn cotton sheet wrapped round the lower half of the body, with another around the shoulders. All the women wore long white plain dresses, with head-coverings and white stockings, but went unveiled. In the steps of the Prophet people had the same value in God's sight. Father told me, with an expression of deep seriousness:

'Once you wear the *Ihram* you've left your old life, and come into your new life. In a way it is your shroud. In this dress, if you die, you'll go straight to heaven, non-stop.'

In the streets, as he went to prayer at the mosque, Father had met an old school friend.

'Attaullah is here. He's a true Muslim – he gives alms to the poor in Pakistan. And he's very religious. This is his third visit.'

The giving of a proportion of one's income for the relief of poverty, known as the *zakat*, or almsgiving, is the Third Pillar of Islam. The Fourth Pillar is the discipline of fasting from dawn to sunset during the ninth month of the lunar calendar, the month of Ramadan. It is after this that the poor-tax or *zakat* is given.

'You're very religious too, Father,' I thought, 'for you give alms and this is your third time also, and who but you has taught me to say prayers.' I looked at his forehead. There, clearly marked, was the depression called the *mihrab*, after the sacred arch of the niche pointing to Mecca in every mosque. This comes through repeated pressing of the forehead to the ground in prayer rituals. One has only to see this to know a man of prayer – and prayer is the Second Pillar of Islam.

I didn't go out at all for the remainder of our first day, but stayed, praying, reading the Holy Quran and otherwise preparing myself for the following day's visit to the Ka'aba, which would be very tiring in the heat, jostled by so many people. Salima and Sema brought food to my room and remained with me.

'There are so many people and yet it's so peaceful,' said Salima, during the evening. The streets were packed with pilgrims, yet there was an air of tranquillity. There was no frantic haste. To be in this place was Paradise – the fulfilment of all desire.

When the *muezzin* called from the minarets of the mosque at sundown, everyone in Mecca stopped where they were, and turned toward the Ka'aba, the potent symbol of unity for millions of Muslims in the four corners of the world. They stood upright, hands open on each side of the face. 'God is most great,' they prayed. The arms were lowered and the right hand placed over the left arm, above the waist for a woman, below for a man. 'All Glory be to Thee, O Allah! and Praise be to Thee; blessed is Thy Name and exalted Thy Majesty; and there is none worthy of worship besides Thee.' There followed some other prayers, the *Fatiha*, some verses of the Quran, then *Allahu Akbar*. At this the worshippers bowed from the hips, hands on knees: 'How glorious is my Lord, the Great!' They stood erect, hands at side: 'Allah has listened to him who has praised Him; Our Lord, praise be to Thee.' Then saying '*Allahu Akbar*' they prostrated themselves: 'All glory be to my Lord, the Most High' (three times). Then they raised themselves and knelt in a sitting posture: 'O Allah! forgive me and have mercy upon me.' They prostrated themselves again. This was one complete *Rakat*, which was to be followed by some repetitions of the movements and prayers.

As a sick person, I performed the sacred ritual, with the assistance of my maids, sitting, the arch, or *mihrab*, on my prayer mat pointing towards the Ka'aba.

Would I wake from this mystic dream in my own room at home, or was I really saying my prayers here at the centre of the world? Tingling anticipation shot through me, a heady excitement. 'To be here O God is enough, even if I cannot walk.' To see with one's own eyes the House of God, built by Abraham, was a gift that one could live on for the rest of one's days.

'It's true you've lived 14 years as a crippled person,' I told myself, 'But here, where faith is strongest, where so many prayers are centred, God will hear your family's prayers, and Mohammed will ask Him to heal you.'

When I thought of God no picture rose to mind, for how could one make a picture of the Eternal Being? He, though called by more than ninety-nine names in the Holy Quran, was still unknowable. There was nothing human to which He could be compared, so I had been taught. But my lips moved in the words of the long-cherished *Fatiha:*

*'You alone we worship, and to You alone
We pray for help.
Guide us in the straight path,
The path of those whom You have favoured . . . .'*

To the Muslim life is a road, and every individual is somewhere on that road between birth and death, creation and judgement. I too had entered on a Pilgrimage which, though I couldn't forsee the end, would last till the end of my days.

Next morning we were all up before dawn, and after prayers and early breakfast we started on the walk to the Ka'aba. Father had arranged for me to be taken in a wheel chair, while my maids walked alongside, and he strode in front. Many sick and elderly were being carried in this fashion. I sat propped up, enjoying the scene, which was one of great liveliness, as thousands of men and women of all ages and all nationalities together pressed towards the House of God. I had never before in my life seen so many people in one place, so determined on one object – not even in Lahore, or Rawalpindi, when Father took me there in his car, not even in London. The human tide surged forward with one aim, one end, praying as they walked, or reciting the rhythmic, lilting verses from the Quran.

Massive outer walls pierced by gates surrounded the ancient Haram mosque. Before entering we had to submit to a body search by men and women stationed at the gates. Father had warned me about this:

'It's rumoured that infidels have tried more than once to penetrate into our holy places to do some mischief, and to defile them.'

'What happened to them, Father?' I enquired fearfully.

'Oh, I expect they were shot,' he said. I shivered at the punishment, but felt they deserved it for the insult.

We entered a great arena, dominated by towering minarets. In the centre of this stood the mosque, begun in the 8th century and now greatly extended to take thousands of worshippers. Our party crossed carpets, shoes in hand, and left them in exchange for a numbered ticket. Then we passed through a gate to the inner courts. We found ourselves in a vast open space, in the middle of which stood the huge cube-like granite building known as the Ka'aba, the House of God, draped with black brocade embroidered with the names of God in gold.

The whole open space was white with thousands and thousands of people, all with their faces turned to the Ka'aba. Round the Ka'aba people were walking or running in an anti-clockwise direction.

Marble pathways radiated out from the centre. We walked along one of these, and reached a circular area where I was transferred to a wooden *palki* or litter carried by four stalwart men, before we were swept into the melee of whirling figures. Round the Ka'aba we went, three times running, four walking, I bobbing on my *palki* like a piece of foam on the crest of a tide. Each time we passed the Black Stone on the north-east corner, put there by Mohammed with his own hands, we raised our arms and shouted *Allahu Akbar* – 'God is Most Great!' It was a bumpy ride and I looked anxiously at Father, but he seemed unaware of the heat, the pressure of the crowd or the discomfort. To be here was all he desired.

On our last circumambulation we found ourselves at the Black Stone. I remember I had been told that this was the stone which was thrown down to Adam by God. It was a powerful symbol of our faith, touched by God, Adam and Mohammed. The bearers pushed us forward, and lowered my *palki*. I was helped to lean forward to kiss the Black Stone. It was set in silver and was sprayed with perfume. I shut my eyes feeling in touch with the Prophet. The Stone did not feel like stone at all. It was warm to my lips, and there was a sense of peace around me. I said, 'Please heal me, and heal these others.'

But nothing happened. Salima and Sema pulled me upright and we passed on. I kept my head down, avoiding Father's troubled gaze. We next moved on to the praying place of Abraham and offered a prayer for our dearest wish. 'Please heal me,' I prayed.

The next ritual was to run between Safa and Marwa, two small hills enclosed in the Great Mosque, about half a mile apart. Hagar and Ishmael are said to be buried under these mounds.

'It is a great game,' I thought, but kept it to myself. Laughing would not do here, for everyone else was taking it very seriously. I went back to a wheel-chair to progress along marble pathways between Safa and Marwa seven times, tracing the movements of Hagar as she looked for water for her child Ishmael after they had been cast out. Tradition has it that God opened a spring of water, Abb-a-Zamzam (the Water of Life) near there. People were buying the water and drinking it from metal cups. Father saw that we had a drink and bought a skin of the water to be delivered at the Hajji-Camp. Some of this was to be taken back to Pakistan, the rest was for me to bathe in.

These rituals had taken most of the day without food or rest and we now returned to the Hajji-Camp to await the next event. This was a walk to Arafat, a place about seven miles from Mecca, where Muslims say God tested Abraham by asking him to offer his first-born son Ishmael as a sacrifice. When God saw Abraham's obedience he stopped the sacrifice and instead provided a substitute ram, caught in a thicket. I think that we visited Mina on the way there and back, to throw stones at three pillars, representing the devils who tried to tempt Abraham to refuse to offer his son. Everybody was laughing at the ugly pillars as they threw stones or shoes. To throw shoes was a great insult.

Then we went to the place of sacrifice, just outside the town, and stood in line until we reached the butcher, who knew about our lambs. He held the knife in one hand and the lamb in the other, and I put my hand on the knife, and the butcher did the killing. The blood ran from the neck of

31

the lamb into the trough, and it twitched and shook as if trying to get away. I felt nothing for the lamb – its death was fulfilling the command to sacrifice. Then another butcher came and took the lamb away and skinned it. We could not stay to see all our lambs slaughtered, because the lines were so long, but it was all very well arranged. Our lambs were checked off, and would be offered later. We watched as other people came up in our place to offer their lambs, goats or camels. Up to six people could share in offering a camel, said Father. I was glad we didn't stay long enough to see a camel die.

I knew what would happen to the meat. Father had told me:

'Some of it goes to the poor – they eat well at *Hajj*. Some we will eat at the Hajji-Camp. A lot of it will be burned. It cannot be kept in this heat.'

The pilgrims stayed in Mina for three days, and on the second day resumed ordinary clothes, making the dusty, hot streets blossom with brilliant colour from national costumes. The men shaved their heads or had their hair cropped all over, and the women had at least an inch cut off. Everyone wished each other 'Happy *Hajj*.' These were days of feasting with friends old and new. It was also a time to talk over differences and be reconciled to others.

'The world would be a happy place if we kept the spirit of *Hajj* for the rest of our lives,' said my Father.

We did not, however, stay at Mina, because of my disability, but returned to the Hajji-Camp. Soon after our return, I sat on a stool in the deep bath, supported by Sema, reciting prayers as Salima poured the water from Zamzam over me from a plastic bucket.

I really expected at that moment to be healed, to have all this paralysis taken away. But nothing happened at all. My body was as heavy as lead, still. My heart was heavier as my servants lifted me, and dried me, and dressed me.

In a little while Father, who had been waiting in the next room expecting me to walk through the door on my two legs, came in to see me.

'Today it was not the will of Allah. But we will not give up hope. God is Most Great,' he said, then went quietly out.

After these rituals many of the *Hajji* would return home, to be respected in their own countries. Some people would even put *Hajji* before their names, or put it in their shop signs to show they were honest. 'I'd like to believe it about some of them,' said Father, with the merest hint of a smile.

Many, like us, were going on to Medina, the second important city for Muslims, 250 miles away, where Mohammed lived for 10 years after he was driven from Mecca and where he set up Islam in 622, beginning the Muslim Era. He lived there for the last part of his life, and we were intending to see his Mausoleum. Many stories which so thrilled me as a child centred round this city.

The Mosque at Madni is magnificent. We walked on thick, beautiful carpets and paid our homage at Mohammed's tomb. It was covered and carpeted and surrounded by glass. People walked round it and kissed the tomb through the glass with flying kisses. They also threw in money, and wreaths of flowers. The attendants picked them up and decorated the tomb.

Around the courtyard people sat and sang religious songs. Since Father was a *Pir* he asked if I could be allowed near to Mohammed's tomb. The attendants opened the door for me and I sat by the door in a wheel chair for two or three minutes and prayed. It was a marvellous experience. We visited other tombs in the area, then we finished by visiting Fatima's date garden. Mohammed made it for his daughter. We bought a basket of 15 kilos of the dates (very expensive) to share with the family at home.

At Medina we said goodbye to Qazi. Father gave him some *baksheesh* as a gift in an envelope. He had been pleasant and helpful, and we were quite sorry to see him head the car homewards to the Sheikh, carrying our salaams.

From Medina we flew to Bethel Mukkoudus (Jerusalem), which we found full of pilgrims of three faiths, Muslim, Jewish and Christian. Our Pilgrimage, which varies its time every year, by ten days according to the moon, this year happened to coincide with the Jewish Passover and the Christian Easter. The Mosque in Jerusalem is called *Al-Masjid al-Agsa*, the Farthest Mosque, towards which the Prophet Mohammed prayed before Mecca became his centre.

The Dome of the Rock right next to it is linked with Abraham. David bought it and Solomon built his temple here, which Titus destroyed, and here the prophet Jesus walked and talked. Today the Jews wail by the remaining wall for their lost glory.

We only stayed for one night at a hostel near the Dome of the Rock, and I didn't visit it, as I was feeling too upset about not being healed.

We left next day for Karbala, in Iraq, to see where the grandson of Mohammed, Hussein, and his family and servants, consisting of 72 people, are buried. This was a scene of a terrible battle, when Hussein and his brave 72 went against Khalifa Yazid of Syria, and were martyred. Since then we Shia Muslims have always remembered the anniversary of his death, with mourning processions in the streets when men and boys go along lashing themselves. In the month of Moharrum people wear black and no one, in a city like Jhang, would think of arranging a family wedding.

We prayed for healing at Karbala, but none was given. We had been on Pilgrimage for one month and it was time to go home. As we waited for the plane to Karachi Father looked down at me.

'God is testing you and testing me. Don't be hopeless. Maybe at some stage in your life you'll be healed.'

Dear, good Father, so patient, and faithful. He was trying to encourage me, and it had the desired effect. My wilting faith revived.

I said, 'All right. I won't be hopeless. I'll remain faithful to the Prophet and to Allah.' And I laughed, to show I didn't really mind going as I came.

He stooped and kissed me. 'I was expecting this from you,' he said.

The servants too whispered, 'Bibi, just wait upon Allah.'

So we flew back to Lahore, via Karachi, feeling that some special compensatory blessing would attach itself to me because of the Pilgrimage, but aware that we had to wait the time of Allah for it to be revealed. We were met at the airport in Lahore by our family, and by our servants. They brought garlands of sharp-smelling orange and yellow marigold flowers to put around our necks. They all touched us and called out *Allahu Akbar*, for it was a blessing to touch a *Hajji*. They looked at me, still crippled, but made no comment.

Father said to my brothers and sisters:

'God isn't an unjust God. We must have the patience to wait God's time.'

'That's right. Our sister must have the patience to wait.'

We stayed overnight in Lahore in a bungalow owned by one of the family and travelled back next day in a convoy of cars, to be greeted by the rest of the household with a joyful welcome.

4: The wedding

To return from *Hajj* was almost as exciting as going there.

'Let me touch you,' said Samina, and wanted to hear, over and over, all we had seen and done. It was like this whenever pilgrims returned from Mecca. Crowds of people in Lahore would run to the station shouting '*Ya Mohammed,*' and '*Ya rasool Arbi,*' and would try to touch the *Hajji* as they came off the train from Karachi. Thus they would get free some of the blessings which others had acquired at such great cost.

The excitement lasted a month, during which time relatives travelled from far and near, and people of the city came too, bringing little presents – this being a tradition of the homecoming. Relatives and special friends received our bottles of holy water from the spring of Zamzam. A bottle went to the maulvi, who came to see Father to discuss the Holy Quran and the *Hadith* for many hours each week.

As for me, 'God bless you,' everyone said, with new meaning, because I had been on *Hajj*. What we all wanted, of course, was my healing, but that hadn't been granted. If there were under-currents of criticism about this, none reached me. The family merely sighed and kissed me and said 'God will heal you in the future, Bibi-ji. We must bow to His will.'

So although there was this real sadness in my heart, at the apparent failure of our purpose, in other ways there was growth. I had seen more than many in our city, where people could save all their lives and still not have enough money to go on pilgrimage. That intensity of feeling I had witnessed at the Ka'aba remained with me, making me dimly aware that for some there was a journey – like the Sufi 'journey of the heart' – of which the pilgrimage to

Mecca was an outward symbol. The goal of those travellers was that they should be utterly submitted to the divine Will – Islam means 'surrender.' I would not have put it so neatly at 14, yet I remember how strong the certainty grew that I should keep away from everything that would contaminate me, in order to devote myself more and more to prayer.

When the *azzan* sounded, it was with a clearer intent that I bowed, on my prayer mat with the arch turned to the Ka'aba and Salima supporting me. It wasn't only because of what I had been taught, but because of a felt need. At different times during the day, knowing of no other way to offer the prayers of my heart for a healing touch, I passed through my fingers the string of beads brought back from Medina, repeating the word *Bismillah* (the name of God) with every bead. But with no means of knowing God's will in the matter, and there being no improvement, I went on praying my mechanical prayers, and looked set fair to do that for the rest of my days.

After all the excitement of the month after our return, July was quieter. I think Father was depressed about me. Suddenly he said, 'Let's have a wedding.'

'Oh Father' – I could have danced with delight. I loved weddings. One of my earliest recollections, if not the earliest, was of my oldest sister's wedding to a cousin when I was four years old. Anis Bibi was 14 at the time.

I remembered the red dress she had made for me, of the same material and colour as her own. Hers was richly embroidered with gold, and she wore fine jewellery in her hair, with a crown and a pearl-encrusted nose ring. On the right hand she wore five rings attached by a *punjangla* to bracelets round her wrist, and over all a *dupatta* made of the finest silk gauze. I sat on her knee almost the whole time, and she held me tightly and protectively, hugging me as I sometimes hugged my doll. When the maulvi came in to say the words of the marriage over her, I felt her tremble, and I patted her cheek, under the veil, to find it was wet with tears.

All the male guests were with the groom next door, and all the female ones with us. The bridegroom, as was our custom, had never seen his bride's face, except when they were young and unaware, but no matter. He would love her. Everyone loved Anis Bibi, who so resembled our dead mother.

It was a big wedding. Some top-level people came. There were many presents. The dowry we gave was rich and it must have beggared Father. Twenty-one of everything went with Anis Bibi to her new home along with money, gold, presents for the groom's relatives . . . a fortune. Everyone said it was the best wedding the town had ever seen.

When Anis came to say goodbye to me I clung to her and sobbed. She was all the mother I knew.

'I will come and see you often,' she said. In fact she would return the next day, as was our custom, to remain in the parental home for a few days before leaving to take up residence with her in-laws. There would be visits back and forth for some time, until the young people were judged old enough to set up on their own.

Safdar Shah's wedding took place at the bride's home, and it was the reverse of Anis's. Our women did not attend. We waited till they brought Zenib the bride back to us on the next day, with her splendid dowry. She stayed two days then went back to her parents' home for a week. The couple had been engaged since childhood but had never seen each other, as was customary, but other things were changed. The bride was older, 18 at the time. She stayed with us while Safdar Shah completed his business studies at an American college, before going into business in a packaging factory in Lahore. Then they went to live in Samanabad and had a nice bungalow of their own.

I liked having her with us. She spent time with me in my room, or sat with me in the swing seat in the women's half of the garden. There I was wheeled daily when the weather was suitable, to sit among the roses and sweet peas, the orange and mango trees, and be lulled by the splashing of little fountains.

When we were there the gardeners kept well away, for an invisible line divided us from them.

After this, in quick succession, Samina was married and went to live in Satellite Town, Rawalpindi, with her husband's family. Then it was the turn of Alim Shah. He had just graduated in law studies and he went to live at Samanabad with his new bride, and became an official of the Gas Board.

My marriage was of course impossible. We released my cousin from the engagement and he eventually married a very nice girl cousin from another side of the family.

So Father and I were left at home, and there began a precious period of my life, when I had his company in a much closer way than before. All his children were settled, and he was at rest in his mind. When the time came to render his accounts before God he would not be held to have failed in his duty. There was between us all a very deep bond, compounded of familial affection and religious faith. Our inspiration and example came from Father.

There were two other members of the household that I have not mentioned. Uncle and Aunty. They had arrived after Partition in 1950, the year before I was born. Many people were made homeless on both sides and Father, as was his duty, advertised in all the papers for any Sayed family in that position to come forward.

In due time, this couple arrived from Karachi and became part of the family. 'Uncle' became an honorary 'brother' and was helped to set up in a small wholesale business by my father. 'Aunty' helped to run the household after my mother died, and took charge of me.

I liked them – they were nice and polite – and I was diverted from the emptiness of the house by their two children, a boy aged 12, and the girl, who was eight.

Aunty was a good-hearted woman, very grateful for the roof over her head, but obsessed with the sufferings her family had endured at the birth of the Pakistan nation.

'It was terrible, terrible. I saw my own brother murdered before my very eyes . . . oh, you don't know how we suffered. They burned our home . . .' and here she broke off, overcome by pain.

Gradually that sad experience took second place to the bright future she saw opening up for her children. Her daughter was being educated, like her son. 'She'll be a doctor,' said Aunty proudly. 'Abas, he'll go into the Army.'

These were respectable occupations. For girls especially, the modern trends in education produced problems. What could they do? There were a few careers open to women, some of whom, especially if living in the large cities, were getting ideas which conflicted with tradition, which was interested in seeing girls married and into homes of their own as quickly as possible.

'Don't you think so?' said Aunty.

I pulled myself back from my reverie. 'Perhaps so,' I said.

'Oh yes indeed,' said Aunty. 'My daughter should finish her studies, and qualify as a doctor. Think how useful it will be when she marries and her children are sick.'

I didn't mind her rattling on like this for an hour or so at a stretch. It was really only necessary to make a comment now and then to keep the flow going. It was a harmless amusement for her and it enabled me to think of something else.

Aunty and Uncle spared me many fretting worries to do with the servants, for like every household we had a number of these who had to be overseen, and for whose welfare we were responsible.

Salima had been with me since I was seven. She was a shy village girl of 14 when she took over my care. As I grew older, she was given an assistant, Sema, who came from the same family.

We had other servants who were organised for us by the *Munshi,* or clerk, from his office, near the front entrance to the bungalow. He took his orders each morning from Father. He saw that the shopping was done, that the menus were arranged to suit the occasion, that supplies were ordered, that letters went to post, that visitors were properly received, that bills received attention, and that a proper account of his stewardship was rendered each week. Lower down the chain of command, but quite a character in his way, was *chowkedar*, the gatekeeper. When visitors rang the bell at the gate it was *chowkedar's* responsibility to find out what business they had with us, and if judging them honest, pass them to Munshi, who would then conduct them to the correct member of the household.

There were four gardeners; Dita was the chief – he supervised the buying of plants and the digging of holes to put them in and the setting out of pots of plants – in the sunny garden in the winter and in the shady verandah in the summer. There was a second gardener, who saw that Dita's orders were carried out; a third looked after the tube well to see we had water for the garden and for the little fountains splashing in the garden. Dita's son cut the grass and kept everything neat.

We had a male cook and his assistant. I never went into the kitchens – that invisible line prevented me. Rahmat Bibi was the dairymaid – she made the butter fresh every morning from our buffalos' milk. Lahraki brought the food to the table and Sati assisted. They also did the housework.

Thus power and responsibility filtered through many channels, and their interests and ours coincided. Wages were not high, because most of the servants lived in the compound and had food and clothing. They did not work as hard as people outside – or so I thought then.

I would never shout at my servants, and I was glad to see that Aunty, for all her scolding, did not shout either. I did once hear an altercation with the *dhobi*, or washerman, who had lost some precious garment. It always amazed me how these dirty clothes would in a week be transformed to snowy whiteness, be made smooth with a charcoal iron, and brought back with never a crease – and all out of a mud house with only a hand pump nearby for running water or the irrigation canal to wash in.

Dhobi would never be rich, but in many ways he lived well. He was not paid in cash but in kind – wheat, a bag of rice. What he did not consume he bartered out in the villages for the things he needed.

41

'It's not a bad life. I hope I could live as well if I lost all this,' said my father spreading his hands around to indicate his comfortable house and land.

Father had distinct theories on work in a culture such as ours. 'Of course we have many servants looking after few people, but they do not cost much to feed and clothe. They need us as much as we need them. I defy any developed country to find a better system for feeding and occupying its poorer classes.'

I had a teacher, Razia, who came to steer me through the intricacies of Islamic Religious Knowledge, Urdu, history of India and Pakistan, maths, Persian, basic science. In place of English I took Advanced Urdu.

Razia was a kind, thoughtful woman, tall and beautiful. She came into my room like a breath of air, and thanks to her I took an interest in the world around me, listening to the news on radio, and religious programmes, and watching the television set, which Father bought after our visit to Mecca to soften the disappointment of my homecoming.

One day Razia said: 'You are now ready for the examinations. I shall soon not be able to come any more to teach you.' I was so excited at the prospect of the examinations that I didn't fully comprehend how much I would miss our lessons.

I passed my matric and then I sat all day, with nothing to do. Razia had another pupil, and couldn't come to see me often.

Father, however, continued to come in every evening and he would sit and read the newspaper and tell me news of the day concerning the business, and news of happenings in the town. Occasionally we went on trips. Once I had thought of our area as the centre of the Punjab – which of course was the centre of Pakistan. Apart from the quality of its breeding animals and its growing industrial life it was also a famous centre of romantic interest. There was a tomb there of a young couple who were separated by life but united in death.

I heard the story first from Samina, in all its tangled detail, and afterwards Father took us to gaze at the white marble tomb which commemorates the ill-starred lovers.

It concerned Heer, whose name means 'beautiful,' and Ranjha, the farmer's son who wanted to marry her. A question of caste was involved, though both were wealthy. Heer's parents tricked her into marriage with the husband of their choice, but she still loved Ranjha, to whom she had become engaged. Eventually the king got to hear of this, and dissolved her marriage. But her *doli*, the wedding car, taking her to Ranjha, proved to be her hearse. Her uncle gave her a poisoned drink as she left the home. In true Romeo and Juliet tradition, Ranjha committed suicide.

Such stories fed our passion for romance. Not until much later did I compare it with my father's feelings for my mother. That was no airy, romantic passion but a whole-hearted love that made him sacrifice himself for her, alive.

5: Death's sting

I don't like remembering what came next, although the sting of memory brings with it consolation. Our father, always so strong, fell ill.

It was December, 1968, and there was heavy rainfall, and cold weather. Father spent too long out on his estate in the country and came home soaked and chilled. That evening he went to bed with a fever.

Next morning he struggled to his office, grey-faced and sweating, conducted his business and came home again. That evening he was worse, with a strange rasp in his breathing.

The doctor came and prescribed medicine. The mullah came also and said prayers. The fever went down and Majeed took him to work once more, then brought him home again in a state of collapse and fighting for breath.

The close family gathered around and we bent our wills to help him fight the sickness, which was now diagnosed as pneumonia. Father should have been in hospital, but he insisted on staying at home, and kept trying to work from his bedroom. For two or three days he struggled. Then the change which we all dreaded took place. He was losing the battle and we were powerless to save him. He began to give us messages and instructions about the disposition of his property, and he handed over the deeds to Safdar Shah, who held his power of attorney.

Father thought of me, even in his extremity. He looked at me and gasped with a great effort: 'I have left you a lot of property. Even if you keep 100 servants you will not be a burden to anyone. Look after uncle and aunty and give them whatever is necessary.'

We stared at one another in terror. 'This isn't happening,' we cried to each other. He was slipping from our grasp, like water sinks into the earth, not to be recalled except by the sun.

I was in my wheelchair at his side and I leaned over him, distraught.

'Father, don't leave us. We need you. If you go I'll follow you,' I wept, hardly knowing what I was saying.

He opened his eyes and weakly laid his hand on my head:

'This is a burden for you, but you mustn't commit suicide. It's a sin. Don't ever forget you belong to a Sayed family, the family of Mohammed. You will go to Paradise – so don't commit suicide or you will go to hell. Don't listen to old wives' tales. Live a righteous life and we will all be together with your mother.'

Here he raised himself slightly and he grasped my arm feverishly, his eyes glittering with a strange, fixed light, as if seeing a vision. He gasped out, 'One day God is going to heal you, Gulshan. Pray to Him.' Then he fell back on the pillows, breathing heavily and slowly. His eyes closed.

I remained there weeping bitterly. 'How can I have faith, if you're not with me, Father?' I sobbed out.

Safdar Shah then started to cry:

'Don't leave us. We still need you. You are our mother and our father.'

I looked at my brother, the hard business man. I had not realised that he had such tender feelings in him for this man who had brought us up and cared for us through childhood and youth.

Father's eyes opened. He was making a supreme effort of will to stay with us.

'Look after your sister,' he said to each of his children in turn, and they made a solemn promise. Then he drank some water, said a few verses of the Sura Ya Sin in which we joined – and closed his eyes for ever. He remained like that, breathing heavily and slowly for several hours, while we watched beside him; then at 8 am on December 28th,

1968, he died, while his friend the maulvi was reciting the Sura Ya Sin.

> *'And when the Trumpet sounds, they shall rise up from their graves and rush forth to their Lord. "Woe to us!" they will say. "Who has roused us from our resting place? This is what the Lord of Mercy promised: the apostles have preached the truth!" And with one shout they shall be gathered all before us.*
>
> *'On that day no soul shall suffer the least injustice. You shall be rewarded according only to your deeds.*
>
> *'On that day the dwellers of Paradise shall think of nothing but their bliss. Together with their wives, they shall recline in shady groves upon soft couches. They shall have fruits and all that they desire . . . .'*

We read this traditional passage through our tears, believing it would ease the physical passage of death for our father. Then Samina kissed his dead face, and we all followed her example.

For the next few hours he belonged to the males of the family and to neighbours, skilled in the rituals of death. They and the servants washed the body and dressed Father in a special white shroud, which he had brought back from *Hajj*, ready for his departure on the final journey. It consisted of a long shirt and two sheets to be wound around the waist and across the shoulders. They put a turban on his head, and wrapped him in an enveloping white sheet, placing him in a box, which had prayers and verses from the Holy Quran written all around it. This was left open for six hours for the women of the family to come and pay respects. Later the box was placed outside in the garden, while the mourners walked past in a never-ending stream, each one bending to kiss the box and recite a prayer, or giving it a flying kiss of respect.

Father was an important and well-known man, a religious teacher, a *Pir*, with his own *murreeds* (followers), as well as a prominent landowner and business man. His funeral that evening was as much the concern of the community as of his family. One thousand people attended including family, members of the business community, religious representatives and many scores of *murreeds*. It was a notable funeral.

As a Sayed family we had our own special part of the town graveyard, and here Father was laid, in a small mausoleum where his wife lay buried. Only the men went to the funeral. The maulvi led the prayers and everyone bowed down and prayed. Then the box was lowered into the ground and the mourners sprinkled dust on it. A *chador* or sheet of flowers strung together, was spread upon it.

As for me I was frozen with grief, immobile. Salima and Sema bustled in and out, supervised by Aunty, to wash me, change me, bring me hot milk and massage my head to ease the aching. I was dimly aware of the guard being mounted outside the door. 'No, she doesn't want to see anyone. It's better to leave her alone just now.' Even family members were turned away from my door.

I must have slept, because when next I was aware, it was 3 am by my clock, and I lay still for a few moments, listening for the small sounds which would tell me that the house servants were up, preparing for the day. We had experienced the worst thing in our lives, and yet the routine must go on. 'It's wrong that I should be alive, a useless cripple like me, and he is dead,' I thought. 'God, I can't live like this for perhaps another 30 years. Please take me to Father.'

Why was God so far away, and so silent? Perhaps my forefathers had sinned terribly. Perhaps God wanted to see more patience in me . . . yes, but I had had patience, and I was still sick. If He would not help me I would have to find some way to rid myself of this wearying body. But how? Hang myself? With one hand that would be impossible. Poison? Where would I obtain it? If I could find a knife or scissors . . . they were locked away. Even as the thought was voiced another thought took its place: 'You will never be with Father and Mother in Paradise if you take your own life.' As a Sayed I had automatic right of entry, even if I failed to observe the Five Pillars of Islam, but a suicide could cancel that right.

Perhaps, then, I would never be healed. My heart felt as if it were being squeezed, and the tears flowed unchecked. It was then, out of sheer helplessness, that I began to talk to God, really talk to Him, not as a Muslim does, using set prayers, approaching Him across a great gulf. Driven by a vast emptiness inside I prayed as if talking to One who knew my circumstances and my need.

'I want to die,' I said. 'I don't want to live any more and that's the end of it.'

I can't explain it, but I knew I was being heard. It was as if a veil had been lifted between me and some source of peace. Pulling my shawl around me closely against the cold I spoke more boldly in prayer.

'What terrible sin have I committed, that You have made me live like this?' I sobbed. 'As soon as I was born my mother was taken away, and then You made me a cripple, and now You've taken away my father. Tell me why have You punished me so heavily?'

The silence was so deep and still that I could hear the beating of my heart.

'I won't let you die. I will keep you alive.'

It was a low, gentle voice, like a breath of wind passing over me. I know there was a voice, and that it spoke in my language, and that with it came a new freedom to approach God the Supreme Being, who until then had not given me any indication that He even knew of my existence.

'What's the point of keeping me alive?' I queried. 'I'm a cripple. When my father was alive I could share everything with him. Now every minute of my life is like 100 years. You've taken away my father and left me with no hope, nothing to live for.'

The voice came again, vibrant and low.

'Who gave eyes to the blind, and who made the sick whole, and who healed the lepers and who raised the dead? I am Jesus, son of Mary. Read about Me in the Quran, in the Sura Maryam.'

I don't know how long this exchange lasted – five minutes? A half hour? Suddenly the morning prayer call sounded from the mosque and I opened my eyes. Everything looked normal in the room. Why had no one come with my washing water? It seemed that I had been granted a space of peace and privacy for this strange encounter.

Later in the day I almost convinced myself I had been dreaming, when, with my sisters and other female members of the family, I visited the graveside. All was quiet and peaceful there and fresh flowers had been placed on the pile of brown earth. But I looked at it with horror. He who never would allow a speck of dust to touch him while alive was buried under that dirt. It was too horrible to contemplate.

When we returned from this melancholy visit, it was to keep a mourning period of 40 days. During this time Safdar Shah and Alim Shah would neglect their work while a constant stream of people from far and near, important and humble, visited us and paid their respects to our father's memory.

All this time our food would come from our neighbours. No cooking fires were to be lit in our house. We were expected to give all our time to remembering the dead and talking about him to all who came. Our visitors sat on the floor to show respect and talked about the good things the dead one had done, so honouring his memory and cheering the family. It was a gentle custom, allowing grief proper expression, and bringing the support of the community to the aid of the bereaved family.

After our return from the graveyard, in a state of deep depression a strange thing happened. One of the maids suddenly screamed, and pointed to a chair.

'I saw him sitting there,' she cried. No one was surprised. The sense of the dead person's presence doesn't immediately leave the house, and in my father's case we still couldn't believe he had gone. It was as though he had just stepped out to give the gardener some order and would be in directly. I looked at the maid and wondered why she had been the one to see him.

49

Aunty came in to my bedroom and sat with me for a while, massaging my head to relieve a painful headache which had come as a result of all my tears. 'Your uncle and I will look after you like your father and mother. Please regard us as such and try to look upon this loss as something willed by God. He has taken your Father to Paradise.'

When she had gone, for the need of something to do to take my mind off the happenings of the morning, I called for my Arabic Quran and started to read the Sura Maryam. But it was difficult to read the Arabic with full understanding, though its rhythmic lilting verses had made learning by heart easy. Here a daring idea took hold of me. Why shouldn't I read it in my own tongue?

I wrote a note for Salima, and I gave it to her when she came in to change my clothes.

'Please give the bearer the best available Urdu translation of the Quran,' said my note.

'Take this to the bookshop and ask for an Urdu version of the Quran, published by the Taj Company,' I said. 'Get the money from Aunty.'

Salima nodded respectfully and went out. Two hours later she reappeared, with the book wrapped in newspaper.

'Good,' I said. 'Now would you go and make a cover for it.'

That night, when the household was still and silent I unwrapped the green silk cover and took out the Urdu Quran. I held the book in my hand for a moment. I wanted so much to hear that voice again, with its assurance that my prayers were heard and that there was a way of healing and hope. The way to hear it again, I knew instinctively, was to obey its instruction to read. And so, full of curiosity and sadness, and with not the least idea of how momentous an act it was, I said *Bismillah*, opened the book and began to read:

The angels said to Mary: 'Allah bids you rejoice in a Word from Him. His name is the Messiah, Jesus the son of

50

*Mary. He shall be noble in this world and in the next, and
shall be favoured by Allah. He shall preach to men in his
cradle and in the prime of manhood, and shall lead a
righteous life . . . .'*

On the third day after our father died Safdar Shah came
into his own as head of the family. One of Father's turbans
was ceremonially placed on his head by two uncles – and
from then on he was *Pir* in our family, and Shah. He would
be expected to know answers to religious questions. He
would make a good *Pir*. Some who had that title were
uneducated and superstitious.

For the forty days of mourning the house was full of
neighbours, visitors and *murreeds* and their wives. These
had come to serve us, and they meant well, cleaning the
house and serving other visitors with food. They also
brought clothes for the family, which we were obliged to
wear, out of courtesy.

'These clothes are clothes of death, not life. They will
always remind me,' said Anis Bibi, twitching her *shalwar
kameeze* uncomfortably.

The mourning period closed with two activities. The
grave was cemented over, and a stone raised. Everyone was
invited to the traditional end of mourning feast, the
chalisvanh.

A big tent was erected and the catering was handed over
to a local shop. They set up cooking stoves and filled 150
huge pots with rice. Chick pea pilau was served and sweet
rice, and everyone sat on durrees on the ground and ate off
steel plates, with their fingers.

I did not go to it because I hated to be looked at and
pitied for my deformity, but I heard about everything.

Safdar Shah now had to return to Lahore, but before he
did so he came to see me and sat in the chair my father had
so often occupied, looking uneasy. He was holding the
paper relating to my property, which Father had left me. I
knew what he was going to say and I had my answer ready.

'My dear sister,' he began, 'I would ask you to come and

live with us, but for the fact that Aunty and Uncle are here to look after you. As you know, Father left you the largest share of the property. I don't of course object to this in any way, as Father cared for you so much and he thought especially of your comfort and well-being. But since you're a woman of property, you may now live where you wish, including Lahore.'

I interrupted. 'Thank you my brother, but I wouldn't wish to leave this house, where I have been brought up. I don't want to go to Lahore.'

My brother looked at me keenly. 'Is it quite good for you to remain here to brood?'

'I could brood in Lahore too. Here I'm used to everything,' I said. I did not add the other reason – that only here in quiet and privacy could I pursue my search in the Holy Quran for the prophet and healer, Jesus.

'Very well, if that's how you feel, so be it,' said Safdar Shah. I thought he seemed relieved. 'I think in that case we must put into effect our father's wishes as to the handling of the finance.'

It was arranged that Safdar Shah would put money into the bank in Lahore for me to draw out. I, as head of the household, would sign cheques against the Muslim Commercial Bank each month for expenses. I would give money to Uncle for the running of the house. My brother Safdar Shah would visit twice a month to go over the accounts.

'I know that all will be in order,' said Safdar Shah. 'My father placed great trust in your discretion while he was alive.'

So it was arranged to his satisfaction and he left. They all went, one by one, leaving me to a dreary existence, with no close companion, or friend, to share my loneliness, though I was not without companionship.

Aunty came into my room as he left.

'You are very fortunate to have so much trust placed in your hands,' she said. 'When I was your age it would have been thought unbecoming for a woman to know so much

52

about business . . . but your father (may his memory be blessed) treated you like one of his sons.'

She went out again, and as the silence wrapped around me, I opened my Urdu Quran and read again the passage from the Sura 'The Imrans,' which was now so central in my attention:

'By Allah's leave I shall give sight to the blind man, heal the leper, and raise the dead to life.'

There was a great deal more that I did not understand. Many clever scholars had tried to give their interpretations of the prophet Jesus who, this Sura said, was a created being, made of dust, like Adam, yet one who could, by Allah's power, do all these miracles. That he was important I could not doubt, but who was this prophet who knew my need and that could speak to me from out of heaven as if he were alive?

I had lost my dearest companion and an empty life stretched before me. Yet a seed of enquiry and of hope had been planted in my heart. One day, some day, I felt sure I would find out the secret of the mysterious prophet veiled in the pages of the Holy Quran.

6: The car

Father's blue Mercedes stood silent in its garage after his death, shrouded in black sheets, a memorial to the man who had filled our lives with happiness, now gone like a brilliant sun from our skies, leaving us chilled and cold.

It was the car of a man of substance. Father's departure in it each morning for his work was part of our daily ritual. The car itself was splendid enough, but Father added his own magnificence as he sat beside his driver Majeed, whose turban and straight back told the world how proud he felt to be driving such a master.

We children felt proud too, when we were taken anywhere in the car by Father. The boys went to the mosque school in it, and I went with Father as he sought medical treatment for my condition. Sometimes there were sightseeing trips when he took me from my quiet room out on the road to Lahore to visit relatives.

Now his car was immobile. No one liked to drive it, not even my brother, Safdar Shah. Regularly Majeed took off the covers and polished the car's dark blue surface and its bright chrome fittings until everything shone like a mirror. He rubbed the mahogany dashboard and waxed the leather cushions until they gave off a rich smell. He cleaned the engine in the same manner and greased every working part, jacking the car up so that it should not rest on its wheels. As Majeed worked he talked softly, as if to the car. The maids reported all this to me, with little giggles:

'That Majeed, you should hear him. He has lost a screw. He is telling the car: "You are not dead."'

'Be quiet,' I reproved them. 'You should not joke about such things.'

I felt, uncomfortably, that Father would hear, that he would step out of the shadows settling around the bungalow as the dusk came swiftly in, and call for the car to be made ready, and would drive off, as though nothing had happened. As if to underline this one of the maids came running to me one day with the story that she had seen the master walking in the house.

'Did he speak to you?' I asked.

She shuddered. 'No Bibi-Ji. He didn't look at me, just went straight through that door. When I looked in there was no person. The room was empty!'

I did not chide her for an over-active imagination, just wondered why I hadn't been the one to see his dearly loved face.

Yet that car was a symbol of my own useless state. Must the car stay in its garage for ever – an echo of the days gone by? Was I to stay here helpless, living on memories for the rest of my life?

My brothers and sisters had their own lives to live, and though they faithfully fulfilled Father's instructions concerning me I didn't want to feel I was a burden and a worry to them. My gloom conveyed itself to my sisters. Samina asked me about it one day: 'Little sister, what's troubling your mind, and making you look so sad?'

When I told her she said, 'You will never be a burden to us. We love you too much.'

So when one of the black moods of despair came I tried to talk myself out of it as best I could.

'Look Gulshan, you've had a lot of luck in having such a family. You might have been born poor like one of your maids. You might have had a father who didn't love you, and brothers and sisters who didn't care for you. You are quite educated. You have a roof over your head and Father has seen to it that you will want for nothing. Now make the best of your situation. Think about those days at Mecca, when you were so near to God and His prophet. Remember Father's words that God would heal you, and if that isn't enough for you, remember the voice you heard in this room telling you of Jesus the Healer.'

When I weighed all these things in the balance they should have been enough to pull me out of my despair. Each day I rehearsed my blessings, taking the weights off one by one until my spirits could rise. Yet running underneath was the persistent fear – perhaps I would never be healed.

I turned to prayer even more assiduously than before. My days wound on in a regular pattern dictated by the five set prayer times. I woke at three o'clock every morning and prepared myself for *Fajr ki namaz*, the dawn prayer. Then I read the Quran in Arabic until breakfast, which I took in my room.

After breakfast Salima or Sema would change my clothes, and then I would fill in time reading a religious book, or the newspaper, listening to the radio or writing a letter to my brother or sister, and having lunch. This was followed by a rest period, and then the early afternoon prayer time, *Zohar ki namaz*. When Aunty's children returned from school I would be wheeled out to the garden to watch their play. Two hours before dusk it was *Asar ki namaz*, and around two hours after dusk *Maghrib ki namaz*, the evening prayer. Last of all came the night prayer, to which most merit attached, *Isha ki namaz*.

Women were not required to visit the mosque. Instead, we said our prayers softly at home. I would as soon forget my food as cease to say my prayers, though these prayers were done in a parrot fashion. They were a link with Father, a sign that I was keeping the faith. He had taught me that if I was faithful, I would meet him in Paradise, straight after death, when I would have a new body. All the women in Paradise were going to be young and beautiful, so we were taught in the Holy Quran.

But there were deeper, blacker fears underneath which I hardly dared to confront, let alone mention to anyone. God must be angry with me, and that was why He had taken my Father. I was growing afraid of the God we worshipped.

56

He was hidden from me behind a veil of darkness and unknowing.

None of this showed on the surface of life. In many ways my home seemed a paradise at that time. Situated in a green, fertile land, watered by five rivers, the Jhelum, the Ravi, the Indus, the Chenab, with its new dam, and the Satlaj, our city was thought a backwater by people from Lahore. To me it was a shelter from a wide world full of staring eyes and embarrassing questions about my disability. It was also a haven from a world full of disasters, murders, assassinations, into which I need never go to marry or earn a living. Listening to Urdu news programmes coming from the BBC in London, from the newspaper, and from television, I heard about the troubled world outside, and longed for my Father to be there to talk with about all I saw and heard. There were so many things I didn't fully understand, and I had lost the one who helped to form my opinions.

Of course there was still a lot of talking done in the house. I talked to my uncle about the running of the household and about business. I talked to my aunt about her children, about the servants, about the weather, about the flowers in the garden, about the weddings and funerals in the circle of family and friends. I talked to my sisters about their children and all the intimate gossip of family life, and to my brothers also about family matters and occasionally about the world at large.

'There is so much trouble in the rest of the world. Here in Pakistan we have peace. This is "the holy land."' That was their view of it.

Running underneath all this was a constant current of talk with servants – with Munshi, as he came to my partly opened door once a week to call out the accounts he kept so carefully. This was at my Uncle's insistence. Money was slippery stuff, and there were many holes for it to fall through in our household. He did not want to be held accountable.

I talked particularly with my two maids, who had been with me so long and loved me as dearly as I loved them. But even they were unaware of the most secret change which took place in me over those three years following Father's death, as I began to test the ideas which up to then I had accepted without questioning.

At night, after the children had gone to bed, and aunt and uncle had settled in their own room, when the house grew quiet after the last prayer call, that was the time I reserved for my reading in Urdu of the Holy Quran. The passages I sought had all to do with the prophet Jesus. But I found it puzzling. If he was such a powerful healer why was there so little about him in the Quran?

'Aunty,' I said one day, 'do you know anything about Jesus?'

Aunty picked up a trailing end of her scarf and looped it over her shoulder. She said firmly, as if she were reciting words of a once learned lesson:

'He's the only prophet in the Holy Quran who gives eyes to the blind and who raises the dead and who is coming again. But I don't know in which Sura it is mentioned.'

When I tried to show her in the Urdu Quran I met with resistance:

'You're educated. You can read it. But we still stick to our own ideas, as Mohammed told us,' she said. I saw from this that she didn't really want to discuss it, but she must have passed on this exchange to the rest of the family because I was questioned about it in a discreet way, by Safdar Shah.

He came twice a month and stayed a day or so, to check the handling of the household matters, and to see how I was. My sister Anis came every month, and Samina came as often as she could from Rawalpindi, when she would stay a few days. Never was a sister so watched over, and yet so lonely.

Safdar Shah picked up the Urdu Quran.

'I am glad to see that you are still faithful to your religion, Gulshan. Have you given up reading this in Arabic, as Father taught you?'

'No, Brother, I read both in my routine. I read Arabic in

58

the morning and Urdu at night. I want to find out more about its meaning.'

He was happy at that. 'Good, it is quite all right for you to read both, but don't give up reading the Arabic.' And he left under the impression I was burrowing ever deeper into Islam.

'By Allah's leave I shall give sight to the blind man, heal the leper, and raise the dead to life.'

For years I had read the Holy Quran devotedly and prayed regularly, but I had gradually lost all hope that my condition would change. Now, however, I began to believe that what was written about Jesus was true – that he did miracles, was alive – and that he could heal me.

'Oh Jesus, son of Mary, it says in the Holy Quran that you have raised the dead and healed the lepers and done miracles. So heal me too.' As I prayed this prayer my hopes grew stronger. It was strange, because in years of Muslim praying I had never felt certain that I could be healed. I took my beads which I had brought from Mecca and prayed a *Bismillah* after each prayer, and then I added after each prayer, 'Oh Jesus, Son of Maryam, heal me.'

Gradually, my praying changed until I was praying over and over between prayer times, on each bead, 'Oh Jesus, Son of Maryam, heal me.' The more I prayed, the more I was drawn to this shadowy, secondary figure in the Holy Quran, who had power that Mohammed himself never claimed. Where was it written that Mohammed healed the sick and raised the dead?

'If only I could talk to someone,' I sighed, but there was no one. I went on praying therefore to this prophet Jesus, until there should be more light given.

I had awakened at 3 am as usual, and I was sitting up in my bed reading the verses I now knew by heart. Even as I took in the words my heart was saying its litany, 'Oh Jesus, Son of Maryam, heal me.' Then suddenly I stopped and I said aloud the thought that had been forcing itself into my brain:

'I've been doing this for so long and I'm still a cripple.'

I could hear the slow movements of someone getting up to prepare the water for washing, before morning prayer. In a short time Aunty would be in to see me. Even as I was registering that my thoughts were focusing in an urgent way on my problem. Why hadn't I been healed, though I'd prayed for three years?

'Look, you are alive in heaven, and it says in the Holy Quran about you that you have healed people. You can heal me, and yet I'm still a cripple.'

Why was there no answer, only this stony silence in the room, that mocked my prayers?

I said his name again, and pleaded my case, in despair. Still there was no answer. Then I cried out in a fever of pain, 'If you are able to, heal me – otherwise tell me.' I could go no further along this road.

What happened next is something that I find hard to put into words. I know that the whole room filled with light. At first I thought it was from my reading lamp beside the bed. Then I saw that its light looked dim. Perhaps it was the dawn? But it was too early for that. The light was growing, growing in brightness, until it surpassed the day. I covered myself with my shawl. I was so frightened.

Then the thought occurred to me that it might be the gardener, who had switched on the light outside to shine on the trees. He did this sometimes to prevent thieves when the mangos were ripe, or to see to the watering in the cool of the night.

I came out from my shawl to look. But the doors and windows were fast shut, with curtains and shutters drawn. I then became aware of figures in long robes, standing in the midst of the light, some feet from my bed. There were 12 figures in a row and the figure in the middle, the thirteenth, was larger and brighter than the others.

'Oh God,' I cried, and the perspiration broke out on my

forehead. I bowed my head and I prayed. 'Oh God, who are these people, and how have they come here when all the windows and doors are shut?'

Suddenly a voice said, 'Get up. This is the path you have been seeking. I am Jesus Son of Mary, to whom you have been praying, and now I am standing in front of you. You get up and come to me.'

I started to weep. 'Oh Jesus, I'm crippled. I can't get up.'

He said, 'Stand up and come to me. I am Jesus.'

When I hesitated he said it a second time. Then as I still doubted he said for the third time, 'Stand up.'

And I, Gulshan Fatima, who had been crippled on my bed for nineteen years, felt new strength flowing into my wasted limbs. I put my foot on the ground and stood up. Then I ran a few paces and fell at the feet of the vision. I was bathing in the purest light and it was burning as bright as the sun and moon together. The light shone into my heart and into my mind and many things became clear to me at that moment.

Jesus put his hand on the top of my head and I saw a hole in his hand from which a ray of light struck down upon my garments, so that the green dress looked white.

He said: 'I am Jesus. I am Immanuel. I am the Way, the Truth and the Life. I am alive, and I am soon coming. See, from today you are my witness. What you have seen now with your eyes you must take to my people. My people are your people, and you must remain faithful to take that to my people.'

He said, 'Now you have to keep this robe and your body spotless. Wherever you go I will be with you, and from today you must pray like this:

'Our Father, which art in heaven, hallowed be thy name. Thy kingdom come, thy will be done, on earth as it is in heaven. Give us this day our daily bread and forgive us our trespasses, as we forgive them who trespass against us; and lead us not into temptation but deliver us from evil, for thine is the kingdom and the power and the glory for ever and ever. Amen.'

He made me repeat the prayer and it sank down into my heart and mind. It was in its beautiful simplicity, yet its profundity, so different from the prayers I had learned to say from my childhood up. It called God 'Father' – that was a name that clutched at my heart, that filled its emptiness.

I wanted to remain there at the feet of Jesus, praying this new name of God – 'Our Father' . . . but the Jesus vision had more to say to me.

'Read in the Quran, I am alive and coming soon.' This I had been taught and it gave me faith in what I was hearing.

Jesus said much more. I was so full of joy. It could not be described.

I looked at my arm and leg. There was flesh on them. My hand was not perfect, nevertheless it had strength, and was no longer withered and wasted.

'Why don't You make it all whole?' I asked.

The answer came lovingly:

'I want you to be my witness.'

The figures were going up out of my sight and fading. I wanted Jesus to stay a little longer, and I cried out with sorrow. Then the light went and I found myself alone, standing in the middle of the room, wearing a white garment, and with my eyes heavy from the dazzling light. Now even the lamp beside my bed hurt my eyes and my eyelids drooped heavily over them. I groped towards a chest of drawers which stood against the wall. In them I found a pair of sunglasses, which I wore in the garden. I put them on, and was able comfortably to open my eyes to see again.

I carefully shut the drawer, then turned and looked around my room. It was just the same as when I woke up. The clock still ticked on my bedside table, showing that it was almost 4 am. The door was firmly shut and the windows, with the curtains drawn tightly across, were closed against the cold. I had not imagined the scene, however, for I had the evidence in my body. I took a few steps, then a few more. I walked from wall to wall, up and down, up and down. My limbs were unmistakably healthy on the side that had been paralysed.

Oh, the joy I felt. 'Father,' I cried. 'Our Father which art in heaven.' It was a new and wonderful prayer.

Suddenly, there was a knocking at the door. It was Aunty.

'Gulshan,' she said urgently, 'Who is in your room walking?'

'It's me, Aunt.'

There was a little gasp and then my aunt's voice: 'Oh, that's impossible. You can't be treated. How can you walk? You're telling lies.'

'Well, come in and see.'

The door opened slowly and Aunty came fearfully into the room. She stood pressed against the wall in terror and disbelief, her eyes wide open and staring at my radiant face.

'You'll fall,' she said.

'I won't fall,' I laughed, feeling the power and strength of new life coursing through my veins.

My aunt came forward slowly, hands outstretched, like a blind person feeling her way. She drew up the sleeve of my tunic and looked at my arm, plump and healthy as it had become. Then she asked me to sit on the bed and she looked at my leg, which was as whole as the other.

'It looks strange seeing you stand. I have to get used to this,' she said.

She asked me to tell her how it happened.

So I told Aunty, from the beginning, first about Father's prediction, then about the voice in my room on the night after he died. Then I told her about the three years of reading about Jesus in the Quran, ending with his appearance to me, and my healing.

When I got to the part about Jesus saying I was to be his witness, Aunt broke in with, 'There are no Christians in Pakistan for you to witness to and there's no need for you to go to America or England. Your witness should be to give alms to the poor. When these people come to you for food and money, that will be your witness.'

I had not up to then connected the commission given me

by Jesus with going to England or America. Yet his words were still real and present:

'What you have seen with your eyes you must take to my people. My people are your people.'

A prayer began to form in my mind. 'Jesus, where are your people?'

7: Fame

When I was born my parents consulted a *najumi*, who uncurled my tiny fist to trace its lines of fortune.

'Your daughter will be famous one day,' said the man, after studying my palm keenly for a minute or two. My father and mother were pleased and surprised, and no doubt rewarded him handsomely for the information. I mention this because my father subsequently cursed this *najumi* for a thief and a liar, when typhoid struck me at the age of six months, and it appeared that I was to remain a cripple for the rest of my life.

But as I took the first steps of my life in the dawn of that January morning, I achieved instant fame as a walking miracle. I had no idea then that I was taking steps towards the kind of fame that no one in my family would have sought for me.

The servants came running. The females crowded the doorway uncertainly, their mouths round o-o-ohs of wonder:

'Oh Bibi-ji, is it you? Has God healed you after all?'

'Jesus Immanuel appeared to me in this room and healed me,' I said. Out of sight the male servants listened, dazed with wonder.

Aunty flapped them all out of the way, and, stationing my maids on either side of me, hovered anxiously over my footsteps as I walked out of my room, through the house and onto the verandah. She was watching lest I trip on the unfamiliar edges of carpets, the smooth tiles or the rough cement floors. But my mind took control of my body and began smoothly dictating signals to help it come to grips with the dimensions and planes of the physical world. There is all the difference in the world between being a log of wood, lying in one place, waiting for the bonfire, and a living tree, actively creating life for others. I began to find the difference at once, as I stood, bombarded with new sensations of being alive, on the verandah, talking to my uncle.

I watched him from behind my *dupatta*. I was the head of the household, but he had taken care of it all for me. How would he regard this change of circumstance?

I need not have worried. He was delighted.

'For us you are born today,' he said. 'If your father had been alive he would have been jumping for joy. We have the same kind of joy for you.' He had tears in his eyes as he spoke.

I said with heartfelt gratitude, 'Oh thank you, Uncle. Your support means a great deal to me.'

Soon I heard him on the phone to my brothers and sisters. The still-crisp morning air fairly crackled with excitement, as everyone took in the full import of what had happened.

Outwardly I tried to remain calm as I went and sat down to breakfast with the family for the first time and ate without being helped. I was aware of the eyes from all around the table and from the kitchen as I stretched my left hand for sugar or milk and passed things to the children. They were fascinated, and only their mother's sharp, warning glance kept them from asking too many questions.

'You can walk about and see your own house now,' said Uncle as he departed for his work, taking the children off to school at the same time. So for the first time in my life I wandered about the house, looking into every room, taking possession of every square yard of it and meeting with smiles of happiness on all sides. I felt as if I had woken from nineteen years of sleep.

I remember that I took the key of my father's room and spent some time in there alone. It was an extension of Father, giving few clues as to his real thoughts – a double room, simply and plainly furnished with a *charpai*, a beige carpet, two chairs, lightish green walls and curtains. On the walls was a large framed photograph of him, taken when younger, together with some pictures of Mecca and Medina, and there was also his hunting rifle, which he used when out in the fields.

Tears came to my eyes. I felt his presence so near – as if he had just got out of bed, and left the room for a moment and would return. 'See Aba-Jan, your prayers have been answered,' I whispered, looking up at his high solemn expression and then from him to the pictures of Mecca and Medina. He had done the best he could for me – more than many fathers would have felt necessary. Yet a power greater than he knew was at work in the world and I, his feeble daughter, had somehow been blessed and touched and healed by it.

Yet I couldn't find my mother in this room they had once shared. I went into the small room next door, which she had used as a box room. It had become a safe room, where money, jewellery and ornaments were stored. I had never known her, and there was no photograph to tell me what she looked like since no one would think of taking women's photographs in our family at that time, yet I felt her near to me at this moment and I cried bitterly for her:

'Oh *Ma-ji*, if only you were here. Why were you taken away from me at such a young age? Now I have neither you nor Father to rejoice with.'

But my brothers and sisters came to share my joy. Each person had to hear it all, how the night after Father's death a voice had told me to read about Jesus in the Quran. How I had done this for three years and prayed to Jesus more and more desperately until he appeared to me in my room, touched me and healed me. There was real happiness in our home for the first time since my father died.

'We must have a feast and invite our neighbours and friends from the town,' said Anis.

'Yes indeed,' said Safdar Shah, when the suggestion was put to him. 'We must give God thanks for answering our prayers. And to think we thought your trip to Mecca had been wasted. All the time it was God's will to heal you.'

That first day was a learning time for me, when my brain played strange tricks. I would forget that I could walk, and I would ask Aunty if she would fetch me something – say the shawl on the end of the couch. She would rise to get it automatically, just as I would suddenly remember that I was no longer crippled and would reach for it myself.

By the end of the day I was very tired. Physically, the years on the bed of sickness had been wiped out, but I still had the mind of the invalid. It would take time for me to adjust to all the contacts I now was called upon to make with people from the world outside my sheltering bedroom walls. Now I didn't mind people looking at me. My arm and leg were well; not completely normal, since there had been a number of 'experimental' tests and operations carried out over the years, which had tended to alter the growth rate of some toes and fingers. The difference was that I now had the use of my limbs.

Over the next few days there was a stream of visitors, including uncles and aunts from farther away and my sister from Rawalpindi. At the end of a week we had our feast, when the maximum number of people could gather. I told everyone how Jesus had healed me.

My insistence on saying this produced the first sour note in the whole affair, as it made my brothers restless. When they had heard me on this subject for the sixth time Safdar Shah, who felt his position as the religious head of the family, had to speak:

'We would respect you more if you said that Mohammed had healed you. This Jesus is not very important to us.'

'But I can't say Mohammed healed me. It was Jesus and he told me to say so.'

'Jesus has his people in England, America and Canada. These are Christian countries. You are not going there to tell them about how Jesus has healed you, and it would be wise not to broadcast that sort of thing here.'

Safdar Shah said it as a statement of fact. He perhaps didn't mean to make it sound like a threat, but I read into it all the alienation and enmity that we as a family had learned from our father concerning the People of the Book.

The Book in question was the Torah (Old Testament) and the Injeel (New Testament) – the books of Jews and Christians, contained in the Bible. Muslims took the view that Islam was in danger from them, and tried to show that the Quran, though it came later, was infinitely superior, and more correct, setting the other books right. I had accepted this, but now I began to wonder.

Why, if Jesus was not important, had he been able to heal me? Why did the Quran, which claimed to be the ultimate guide to every detail of our lives, manage to say so little about him? Surely this power to heal was the power talked of in the Quran. Surely it came from God. So step by step I was being drawn along by a hunger for the truth. I wanted to read the Gospels for myself, to learn more about Jesus.

If I was discovering the power to differ from my family they were discovering new things about me, and their new relationship to me. As a sister, helpless and sick, I had been a creature without a will to them. They knew where to find me, and how to treat me. They knew I would always be amenable to what they suggested. I had no power of my own – I was totally dependent on them. Now, however, I was a free agent, and, moreover, I was increasingly found to be my father's daughter, with a mind of my own sharpened by an education I would certainly not have had if I had been well. I could sometimes even win an argument with Safdar Shah. He was learning that it can be very difficult to argue with a walking miracle – it has a moral force of its own.

From the very beginning my aunt was insistent that the vision of Jesus meant that I had to give alms to the poor and that they would go and tell others about him. How could I think anything else? In her range of experience there was simply no way in which a Muslim woman could leave her house, her secure family and go out to preach to others.

I took to Jesus this question of who were his people and where were they, and how could I go to them in face of my family's prohibition.

In my inmost heart I knew the answer. It spoke as a voice.

'If you're frightened because of your family, I won't be with you. You have to remain faithful to me in order to go to my people.'

That was what came to me out of the darkness as I knelt on my prayer mat in the night, after the rest of the family were settled.

'My people are your people. You must take my message to them,' said the voice.

I did not tell the family about my voice, but they, sensing the change in my attitude, watched me constantly, and annoyed me with questions.

'You are not going to leave this home are you? You would not go to England or Canada? Do you remember what you said about England when you returned the last time?'

'Why don't you give *zakat* to the poor, instead of going to England? Then they will tell everybody else about your Jesus.'

I already gave an annual *zakat* of 50,000 rupees to beggars at the door. Now, within two or three weeks, I gave an extra *zakat* of 10,000 rupees.

Uncle came to me after this. 'Now you'll be happy. You've done what God asks of us, to give alms. You've done it generously.'

But I was not happy. In a low tone I said, 'But I haven't given myself and that is what He wants.'

I thought he had not heard but there was a sharp intake of breath. 'Listen Gulshan. I think I speak now as if I were your father (may his soul find rest in Paradise). Whatever Jesus wants, you give it to him – land or money; but don't leave your country, your religion and don't give yourself.'

As the days wore on I became aware of new tender shoots of life springing up within. When the muezzin fluted the prayer call from the tower of the mosque I went to my room as usual, thankful to close the door on Aunty's sharp eyes, and that it was not necessary to have the servants help me. I drew apart, not to perform the ancient ritual, but because praying had now taken on depth and intensity as I prayed to God from my heart.

Within two hours of hearing the 'Our Father' prayer I had written down the words. Every word met a need. It was as if it had been written especially for me, and I had no idea that it was a well-loved family prayer of the Christians.

At other times through the day I said the words in the Muslim fashion, taking my beads one by one and passing them through my fingers, click-click-click, and with each click saying the whole prayer. In this way it was possible to pray where and when I wanted to, since, to an observer, it looked as if I were doing *namaz*, the Muslim prayers.

I must have said that prayer a thousand times over the next few days, and each time I found it easier. I had been given a new vocabulary for speaking to God. *'Our Father'* – oh, these were words that made me see God in a new light. He was Supreme Being, yes, but He was also the Father I had lost.

'How good of you to be my Father,' I wept in the night, and felt the inexpressible comfort of love reaching down to me. The old black fear that God was somehow angry with me, departed.

'Hallowed be thy name.' I understood that, for as a Muslim I had been brought up to revere the holy names of Allah found in the Quran. Muslims use the names of Allah with great reverence, adding little verbal genuflections, such as 'May His name be blessed.' The names of Allah have even visual power over the Muslim imagination, being one of the severely restricted forms of decoration allowed in the mosque. The difference now was that I had seen something of that burning holiness for myself.

'Thy kingdom come, thy will be done, on earth as it is in heaven.' I now saw that Jesus was not just a poor, secondary prophet, he was an eternal king, and would be coming again to bring in a heavenly kingdom on earth, as in heaven.

'Give us this day our daily bread . . .' I had never thought of asking God for bread, since all my wants were more than amply met, but it showed that God was concerned about the material needs of the worshipper and he wanted us to depend on Him, as a Father, for them.

'And forgive us our trespasses, as we forgive them that trespass against us.' Forgiveness? The Muslim's prayers are shot through with anxiety about forgiveness. His or her idea of God is of one who punishes with retribution His own followers as well as the evildoer, or the unbeliever. I had even begun to be certain that I had committed some awful sin, to be punished with my illness and the loss of my parents. The only ground of hope was to fulfil in exact and minute detail the essentials of prayers through the day, and to carry out the Hajj for certain reward, together with the other Four Pillars of Islam.

Yet here was no mention of ritual cleansing, only a certainty that for sin to be forgiven it had to be acknowledged before God, and that the one desiring forgiveness had to forgive others. I, with all my impeccable religious upbringing, had never known such certainties before.

'Lead us not into too severe testing and deliver us from evil' . . . I prayed this because it gave me strength to stay true to my vision of Jesus. Only he could save me from the strong pull back to the safety of Islam, which was coming increasingly from my family.

'For thine is the kingdom and the power and the glory, for ever, Amen.' The majestic words were simple but powerful. I had seen that glory, and been changed forever.

Muslims have no mediator with God – although they imagine that Mohammed takes that position – which is why they assume such humble postures when praying. Yet it seemed that I had been given a mediator who had, in turn, shown me a new way of approaching God. As a Muslim I was responsible for my own actions, bad and good, and had to take the consequences. God could conceivably consign me to hell for bad behaviour. But here was a new view of God. To call Him 'Father' was to make Him responsible for my life and happiness, just as my earthly father had been. So I reasoned, and so I prayed, as happy as a child can be when it has been lost in a crowded bazaar, and then found by its father. I longed to know more, perhaps to get a copy of the Christians' book.

If I had looked up from this path I was following, one step after another, I might have seen the storm clouds gathering over my head. Ten days after my spectacular healing I was resting in my room when the storm broke. The family returned in strength, and gathered in the men's reception room with the door shut to put me on trial – at least that was what it seemed like to me.

They put it differently of course. Safdar Shah made a little opening speech:

'We have gathered the heads of the family to persuade you to give up these extreme ideas you have recently acquired. We accept that Jesus has healed you. But when it gets out it won't look good for us. We are a leading Muslim family, and you will bring us into disrepute.'

Supporting my brothers and sisters and their spouses were my maternal uncles and a paternal uncle, and my cousins, together with my uncle and aunt, who were, I discovered, being blamed for allowing this to happen to me.

I said nothing for a long time, and let them talk. Then I said, 'Aren't you pleased that I have been healed?'

'Oh yes,' they said. 'We were very concerned about your healing, but now it has happened don't go round saying it was Jesus who healed you.'

There was a little pause, and then Safdar Shah added, 'For the sake of Islam we can murder you. It says so in the Holy Quran.'

I looked around the circle in our public room. My sisters had tears in their eyes. My aunt and uncle looked pale with shock and fear. My uncles' gray beards wagged as they nodded their heads vigorously, my brothers' eyes were on me as hawks fasten on a prey. I felt the distance between myself and them growing with every second. How could religion breed such hatred that they would rather see me dead, than telling a truth they didn't agree with?

'Forgive us our trespasses as we forgive them that trespass against us.' Here was a truth that had greater power than any of the laws of Islam. I felt no hatred of them at this moment, only a love that would if it could break down these barriers.

My elder brother said, after a short silence:

'If you continue, you will be expelled from the family and from all the comfort you have here. If you go to Christian people we will even harm them. Of course, there are none here.' At the time I believed that also.

I had always been quiet, unassuming, obedient to my elders and they were now bullying me. The old Gulshan would have given in, quite unable to assert herself. But this new Gulshan felt a power within giving a new boldness. I was not afraid of them. Words I had not searched for came to my lips.

'I've listened to you at length, and of course I understand your concern,' I said. 'I can't answer all the points you've made because I am waiting for the answer of Jesus to me. He will tell me what to do next. When I hear the order I'll obey him, and even if you kill me I'll do it.'

There were audible gasps around the room. 'What impertinence,' said the uncles to each other, looking as if they could not believe their ears at such a cheeky answer. I was surprised at myself, daring to defy family strength in this way. Now what would they do? It was a dangerous moment.

I said quickly: 'I promise I won't dishonour the family in what I do, but I must wait until Jesus tells me how to witness. I haven't met any Christian people by the way. I don't know where to find them.'

The men put their heads together. My sisters and my aunt avoided looking at me. They said nothing, for women were not expected to interfere when men were making important decisions.

I wondered if my family planned to kill me then and there. They would have been within their rights to do so. No one would have questioned it . . . except that I was known and loved by many people around us. My sudden death would have needed an elaborate cover-up.

Safdar Shah delivered the verdict:

'OK. We'll wait to see what you do. And we'll pray for you. Perhaps after all you've gone mad.'

It was over for the moment, but I knew they would not rest until I was silenced on the subject of my healing. But to obey them would be to deny what I was convinced my Father had shown me.

'What do You want me to do?' I prayed to Him in perplexity. The answer came two nights later. With a real sense of urgency, I found myself praying simple words – 'Show me Your way, oh show me Your way.'

I looked up and saw a misty pillar, from floor to ceiling. Jesus was inside the mist, the brilliant light I had seen earlier veiled in the mist. I was not asleep, or dreaming.

Jesus said, 'Come to me,' and gladly I rose and went.

He put out his hand and there was a kind of cloth over it. I put my hand out to him. I felt myself lifted off my feet as if I were in the air. I shut my eyes, then I was put down gently on something soft and when I looked I was standing on an open plain, which stretched away in the distance and was green and cool and was peopled with figures, some near and some far. They all had crowns on their head, and were clothed in brightness which hurt my eyes.

I heard words like beautiful music. The people were saying 'Holy' and 'Hallelujah.' That was a new word to me which Muslims do not use. They were saying 'He is the slain lamb. He is alive' and I realised that they were all looking at Jesus.

Jesus said, 'These are my people. These are the people who speak the truth. These are the people who know how to pray. These are the people who believe the Son of God.'

One face stood out in the crowd. I looked closely at this man, who was sitting down. Jesus said, 'Go ten miles up to the north and this man will give you a Bible.'

As I looked at the man, who, like all the people I was watching, didn't seem to be aware of me, the figures faded away and I came back to myself, kneeling in my room amongst all my familiar possessions. I thought over what I had seen and heard and a great sense of excitement rushed over me. I had asked to be shown what to do next and here was the answer – to go and witness to this man about my vision of Jesus and ask him for a Bible. But where would I find him?

Then I remembered something. Razia lived out at Jhang Sadar, and that was some distance to the north of where we lived. At the feast I had arranged to visit her one day soon.

So that was it. Somewhere near her house lived a man prepared to give me a Bible. I would have to go alone. If my family knew they would attempt to stop me. The decision made, I laid my plans carefully, not really aware yet of how irrevocable this step was to be, and of how it would change my life.

8: The Book

Three weeks after my healing I found the courage to put into execution a plan to obtain a Bible. I told Aunty that I was going to see Razia.

'You're taking Salima?' said Aunty, not entirely accustomed to my new way of ordering my life to suit myself.

'No Aunty,' I said smiling. 'I think I'm old enough now to go about without anyone thinking the worse of me. Please ask Munshi to order the car for me.'

Aunty opened her mouth as if to argue then shut it again, firmly. This new Gulshan was less inclined than the old one to care much about people's idle thoughts.

Majeed brought the shining blue Mercedes around and opened the back door with a flourish. The curtains were drawn inside to shield me from prying eyes. Every inch of his bearing, as we purred out of the main gate, proclaimed his satisfaction with this turn of events. A smiling *chowkedar* closed it behind us and we set off.

Razia was prepared for my visit. What she did not know was that I had a call to make. I sent Majeed away, with instructions to return for me after lunch. Then I turned to meet my teacher, who was overjoyed to see me in such good health, and had a number of questions to ask. She was disappointed and a little curious when I said I had to go on to see someone urgently on the other side of the city.

'No, I don't need company,' I said. 'It's just some business I have to transact.'

I left her standing perplexed on her verandah, looking after me as I hurried down the drive and out to the main road. I felt uncomfortable. Never had I tried to deceive anyone in my life before, but this was the only way I would ever get out to obtain a Bible. It was not until I was outside that I realised I had left my *burka* behind – it seemed entirely symbolic of the freedom which was growing inside.

A horse-drawn *tonga* came towards me and I hailed the elderly *tonga-wallah*.

'I am looking for a man who is a Christian who lives on the Kachary Road. Do you know of such a one?'

He looked straight ahead, between the ears of his old horse, as though he had not heard, and I added quickly, 'I have a piece of work to be done.'

He gestured to the north. 'There is a place. A very old place which was there before Pakistan came into existence. I do not know if any Christian lives there, but if you want I will take you.'

'Please take me there.'

I got into the tonga. My tonga-wallah whipped up his lean horse, and we set off at a sedate pace. During the half-hour journey I had time to reflect on what I was doing. What would my sisters say if they could see their beloved, cherished Gulshan travelling on the open road alone in a tonga? There was simply no precedent for it in our family. But I had no choice. Jesus had sent me on this journey and I trusted him for the outcome.

We came to a large building – a Christian chapel, I learned later. Beside it was a big bungalow behind a high wall. The tonga stopped by a gate set in the wall. 'It is here,' said the tonga-wallah.

I paid him and passed through the gate into a compound filled with trees. I went towards the house and saw a man sitting in the sun with a pile of books on a small table beside him.

As I approached the man looked up. My heart leaped with amazement. It was the face I had seen in my vision. Jesus had said, 'This man will give you a Bible.'

The man spoke politely, half rising:

'If you have come to see my wife I am afraid she is not in. She has gone to Lahore.'

I spoke quickly: 'I have not come to see your wife but I have come to see you to get a Bible. I saw you in a vision.'

The man looked startled, and he scrutinised me, trying to penetrate with his gaze the *dupatta* I had drawn over my face, instinctively, as I walked through the garden. Now I let the scarf fall away from my face and looked back at him.

'Who are you? What religion are you? Whose daughter are you?'

'I live ten miles away, and I come from a Muslim family.'

I could see he was frightened at that. What trouble was this strange Muslim woman going to land him in, with her request for a Bible?

He said, 'If I were you I would go home and keep reading your Quran. Whatever is in that is good for you and whatever is in my Bible is good for me. It is not for you to concern yourself with.' He rose to usher me out.

But I remained standing, my heart sinking as the excitement leaked away. I had imagined he would welcome me, perhaps even have been prepared for my visit.

'Jesus Immanuel has sent me to you. Please believe me.'

He studied me for a moment, and then asked me to sit down. I launched into my story, shyly at first, then warming to it, describing to him a little of what my life had been like for nineteen years, as a cripple. I told him about the journey to Mecca, about the hopeful prayers disappointed there. I touched on the tragic death of my father with its amazing result – Jesus speaking to me and pointing me to read the Quran.

He leaned forward intently, his eyes on my face. I had never before been scrutinised by a strange man – except that he did not seem a stranger to me. I went on to tell of the amazing revelation of Jesus in my room, and my healing.

'And then,' I said, 'I saw you. Jesus appeared to me again and showed me his people, and you were among them. He told me to come to you for a Bible. And if you still don't believe me, listen to the prayer that Jesus taught me to pray.' I repeated the words of the 'Our Father' prayer.

When I had finished there was a silence. My friend sat, his arms resting on the arms of his chair, his head bowed on his chest in grave thought.

'Is it possible?' he said, speaking more to himself than to me. He gave a deep sigh and then he rose.

'You sit here for a little while. I have to go and pray about this, as it is a serious step for both of us if I give you a Bible.'

He went inside the house and I sat there in the sunshine, while the hummingbirds darted about the trees, their tiny wings whirring so fast they seemed to be standing still in mid-air.

After what seemed a long time but was possibly not even half an hour my friend came out of the house and said: 'I have prayed and asked the Lord what I should do and He seems to be saying to give you what you desire. But you know that the way you are thinking of adopting is a difficult one, and you could be outcast from your family. You will have to bear a lot and lose a lot, but if you remain faithful you will get everlasting life.'

'I know all that,' I said. 'But this is the way I must go. I want to follow Jesus Immanuel who has healed me and shown me the way of love.'

He smiled and said, 'Now you think about it again. When you give up what you will have to give up for Christ the devil will attack you. He will create a lot of hurdles for you to get over. There will be great opposition. It is even possible that Christian people will create those hurdles for you.'

Tears rushed to my eyes. 'I am not thinking about these hurdles. I only know what Jesus Immanuel has shown me. He has raised me and given me light. I want to know more about him, and he has sent me to you for help. Please help me.'

At this he gave me a New Testament in Urdu and a book called Martyrs of Carthage. Then he prayed a beautiful prayer, which put into words such simple feelings of brotherhood and kindness that it made me feel strong.

From his house I took a tonga again, back to Razia, in time for lunch. I did not explain my journey, but merely said, 'What I went for I have got, but the problem is not yet solved.' Then I changed the subject, and we laughed and chatted as if nothing strange had happened, until Majeed came to take me home.

Aunty had been watching for me. She looked at me intently, but I turned away, feeling certain that what I had just experienced must be written on my face.

'How was Razia?' she asked.

'Well, she has some fine pupils and is happy that her sister is married now.'

'It is a great pity that they have not married hèr off, but I suppose the family has no dowry for her.'

'It is true. She still has to take pupils to help her father, as his business is small.'

Such gossip would have kept us both pleasantly occupied for two hours at least in former times, but the new Gulshan had more important interests.

I excused myself, went into my bedroom and shut the door. Then I lay down on my bed and rested, feeling physically and emotionally drained.

That night I started to read my New Testament secretly. What was it like? Ask a thirsty man what water is like? Ask a baby what mother's milk is like? I who had been fed on husks now found bread for my hunger, and read the truth about human life and destiny written in those pages. Jesus had said to me, 'I am the Way, the Truth and the Life'. His words in the Gospels lit up my understanding. I had never really understood the Quran without guidance. This book was like no other. It opened my spiritual eyes. Its stories came to life as I read. I met the 12 disciples, who had accompanied Jesus in my amazing vision. I found, word for word, the prayer I had learned at Jesus Immanuel's feet. I found the meaning of that precious name given to me in the vision:

'I am Jesus. I am Immanuel . . . God with us.'

I had been brought up to think of God as remote and unattainable. Here at last was the explanation of the divine powers and mission of Jesus – he could raise the dead because he was Lord of life. He was coming again, because he was alive for evermore. He had power eternally because he was God and not just a prophet.

'I am the Way, the Truth and the Life.' I understood it now as a true summary of the Person who was Jesus.

In the course of my reading I came to passages concerning baptism. I read in Mark 1:9-11 that Jesus was baptised. In Romans 6:4 I read: 'Just as Christ was raised up from the dead by the glory of the Father, so Christ was raised to newness of life.'

Newness of life. That was what it felt like to me – as if I had been immersed in fresh, rushing springs of water, bringing tingling life to every part of my being. So this baptism was a sign and a seal on that experience.

As I was musing on this a picture came before me, of a young, sad girl sitting on a stool while her maids poured the water of the spring of Zamzam over her. Zamzam, the water of life, had not washed away my sins nor had it brought life to my dead flesh. Jesus had given me spiritual water of life for my stricken body and my soul. Now I wanted to be buried with him in baptism. I thought about it, not entirely grasping the full force of what I was contemplating, and what changes it would make in my life.

'I have witnessed.' I said to myself, 'Now I have done what Jesus required. I can be baptised and then come back here and live afterwards, can't I?' The question hung in the air, with no voice to confirm or deny it. But my father's face rose up before me, and I felt pain as if a knife had been plunged into my heart.

'Oh Father, forgive me, but I have to follow Jesus, who has healed me.' I spoke aloud in my distress. Immediately a deep peace came upon me and I felt sure that this was the right way to go. Nothing and nobody could stop me now.

By March 12 I had read right through the New Testament. I also read through Martyrs of Carthage. It was full of stories about the early Christians who were thrown to the lions, burned in the fire and treated in other unspeakable ways, remaining faithful. I understood the message being conveyed to me. It didn't change my purpose at all.

The next day I called on Razia again, and from her house went on to the Major as before. Mrs Major was at home this time. I showed them the scriptures I had found.

'There,' I said. 'This tells me I must be baptised. Please will you baptise me?'

He shook his head. 'My daughter, we don't baptise in our denomination.' He looked at me with a strange expression. 'Do you realise what may happen if you do this – you may never be able to return home again. Your family may even try to kill you – oh yes, even as loving a family as yours can change completely when they see one of their number leaving the Muslim faith.'

There was a short silence. I tried to imagine such a state of affairs. To be cast out by my family, even murdered . . . I remembered the family council . . . the hawk-like faces all turned towards me. Then I thought of my father's last words to my brothers – 'Take care of your sister.' Surely, in the end, they would obey that last, sacred command. But even if they didn't, and really tried to harm me, I still must continue following this way. Jesus' words had taken root in my life and there was now freshness, vitality and growth where before there had been the sterility of a religion fixed in the past.

I said firmly, so that they would be in no doubt as to my resolution:

'Jesus Immanuel has told me that I must be his witness, and baptism is the next step for me. I must obey or I will forfeit this peace I now have. Better to die with Christ than live without him.'

The Major exchanged glances with his wife and she gave a slight nod. He turned back to me:

'So be it then. If Jesus has spoken so clearly to you then you must not go against his will. However, it wouldn't be wise for you to be seen going to Lahore with me. My wife will take you on the bus. She has to take our daughter back to school in any case. I'll follow.'

'Certainly I'll be happy to accompany you, Gulshan,' said the Major's lady, leaning forward to take my hands in hers. It was a human touch, welcoming me to the family of my new faith.

So I laid my plans, with little emotion. It might have been another person's life I was so disposing. Islam, it is often said, was born in the desert and its followers learned, in that hard and harsh school, obedience to ends higher than their own. Personal feelings were never regarded as sufficient reason for any deviation. So, in following Jesus, I was able to apply life-long habits of obedience where human feelings might have betrayed me.

Yet, in making my plans, I could not bring myself to completely close the door back to my family. To be honest, I hoped I could go through with the baptism and then return home, to live my own life. An untaught believer, I imagined that the steps I was taking were all that Jesus required of me – to find Christian people and tell them of my healing, and then be baptised.

The Major, however, was seeing farther ahead than I was.

'Don't bring any money and don't bring any jewellery. If you do, it is possible that after the baptism someone may sue the Christians.' He spoke gravely, and I looked at him, interpreting his meaning correctly. He was talking about a clean break, as if I would have to leave everything behind me. Everything? – Money, jewellery, house, lands, family love and support? Could Jesus really want this of me? Had he given me this gift of healing only to withdraw everything else that made life dear?

I told Razia, when I returned to her that day, 'May I come and see you in two days' time?'

'Of course,' said Razia. 'I will be here.'

At home I told Aunty and Uncle that I was going to stay with Razia in two days' time, and we might be going to Lahore.

'I will sign a cheque for 75,000 rupees, so that you can pay all the bills while I am away,' I told my Uncle.

'Where will you be staying in Lahore?' said Aunty, a little frown showing her dislike of this plan. But she could

84

not refuse me permission. I was now a free agent, and, furthermore, the one who signed the cheques.

'Oh, I might stay with my sister and brother,' I said carelessly. 'I will write a letter.'

The next day I asked Aunty to accompany me to Father's grave. She approved of this sign of devotion. We took flowers from the garden and I laid them there with feelings hard to describe. Reverence for his memory mingled with the realisation that eternity was not as he had taught me, a Paradise of material comforts, but the presence of Jesus.

On my last evening I went into my garden, where I had sat so often in my years of helplessness. Standing on the spot where my father's coffin had rested I thought of him again, sadly and long.

The sun sank in a blaze of red, dyeing the walls of the bungalow. I walked among the flowers and fruit and leaves, smelling the mingled fragrances of roses and orange-blossom. A little night breeze rustled the leaves of the orange and mango trees, as the sky above me was swept with purple and midnight blue tints. The moon came up, large as a melon, and stars lay scattered like little diamonds in folds of velvet night. In the bungalow behind me lights had come on, and it glowed, warm and secure. Still I lingered. It was as if I were seeing it for the first time, now when I was to leave it, and I did not allow even the creeping shadows which crouched under the trees to frighten me.

'Why do this? You can be a follower of Jesus without it. You might lose everything by this action.' The thought came drifting out of the darkness. But as if in answer to it a verse I had read came into my mind like a soft voice:

'He that loveth father or mother more than me is not worthy of me . . . he that taketh not his cross, and followeth after me, is not worthy of me' (Matthew 10:38).

I looked again at my house, and I remembered, not just the happy times, but the times when it had seemed to me like a prison, with me, the prisoner, hoping I was on the road to Paradise. I spoke my thoughts aloud: 'Everything

85

changes. But I will always carry this place in my heart.'
Then I left the garden and went indoors to pack.

The next morning I signed two cheques – one of 75,000 rupees I gave to Uncle for housekeeping expenses, so that he would not be short of money and come looking for me too soon – the other, for 40,000 rupees, I intended to give to Razia, to secure her cooperation in my plan. It would leave the door ajar in case I should want to return home.

On March 15, I saw Uncle off to work and kissed Aunty and the maids Salima and Sema, fighting back a few tears.

Aunty said, 'Why are you going like this? Take your car and driver with you to Lahore. How are you going to get around? Are you sure you should go without your maids? Your Uncle is not at all happy about it.'

'Please do not worry, Aunty,' I said, 'I'll write you a letter.' She had to be content with that.

Majeed brought the car around and I got in. I looked back once at the peaceful white house as we rounded a bend, then it was lost to view. The last *chowkedar* saw of me was my hand, waving from behind the curtains in the window of the Mercedes.

I had little difficulty in persuading Razia to fall in with my wishes, when I gave her the money, but I did not tell her the real reason for my odd behaviour . . . that I was buying time, so that no one would prevent the baptism.

'This is for you, because you have been my teacher and have been so good to me. I'm going to Lahore to stay with some friends. I'm independent now and I'm tired of having to explain everything that I do to Uncle and Aunty. I have told my family that you're coming with me, so that they will not worry.'

Razia's beautiful face wore a look of doubt: 'I will do what I can of course to help you, but what if your family come looking for you, and find me here?'

I said quickly, 'Please, if any of them come asking about me, will you pretend to be in Lahore with me? Let your mother go out to see them and you stay inside. I am sorry that I can't explain more than that.'

Razia looked surprised, but she said quickly, 'Of course, Gulshan. Anything you wish. I think we know each other well, and we trust each other.'

I wondered what she would think if she knew my real intention.

I left her as before, and took a tonga to the house on Kachary Road. The Major and his wife welcomed me warmly and I was taken that same day by car to Lahore to a house, run by a minister and his wife who took in converted Muslims, and Rev and Mrs Aslam Khan.

So began a new phase of my life, as a new Christian, among Christian people. It was not at all what I had expected.

9: Baptism

Mr Aslam Khan was a very kind man, who seemed to understand all the problems I was facing. He quickly became Aba-ji (Father) to me. Ama-ji, Mrs Aslam Khan, was kind too, in her own way. A lady, strong-minded and spare of frame, she was always busy about the house and expected me to be busy too.

When I arrived she showed me her guest bedroom, with its simple latticed string *charpai*, and I thought fleetingly of my *palung* at home, with its wide, woven cord base and soft spun-cotton *gada* or mattress.

She said, 'This is your room. These are drawers for your clothes. The bathroom is that way. There is a lot of work to be done because we have so many visitors. You will please excuse me. I have some orders to give to the maid. Whatever you want you must ask the maid for.' And she whisked out.

I did my best to please Mrs Aslam Khan, but I had never done any housework before, so I was stupid and clumsy, and quite unwilling to be criticised for my performance in small tasks I was given. When my hostess came behind me and ran her finger over the ornaments I had just dusted I felt ashamed and angry, but bottled up my feelings inside, where they fermented and spoiled the early days in that home. I wanted to turn to her and say:

'You are right Ama-ji. I have done it badly, but consider that before I came here I never had to do anything for myself. I never washed a dish, dusted a room, made a bed, washed my own clothes, brushed my own hair or even dressed myself. This was not only because we had a lot of servants, but because I was on my bed, helpless, for so many years.'

But I said nothing of the sort. It would only sound like excuse-making and what would be worse in her eyes, pride. She might have answered that I was alright now, and therefore should try to learn, or that I was really dreadfully lazy. So I endured a few sleepless nights, and a mocking whisper in the dark of my room.

'It's not too late,' said the voice. 'Your brothers and sisters are crying. Why don't you go back?'

I saw my uncle and aunt's faces looking down sadly at me. Unable to rest I got up and prowled about the room, until the battle to silence the whispers got too much and I cried to Jesus:

'I have surrendered myself to you and I feel I am on the right path, as you have shown me. Why are these faces appearing to taunt me?'

Then came a still, small voice: 'I am always with you. They can't harm you.' Then I found peace as the words of Jesus filled my mind, and drove away the taunting whispers.

After a week or so the troubles began to cure themselves. I was more active than I had been at home and so I slept better, at any rate the *charpai* ceased to be hard. I read something that changed my attitude completely to all forms of domestic work:

'So he got up from the meal, took off his outer clothing, and wrapped a towel around his waist. After that he poured water into a basin and began to wash his disciples' feet, drying them with the towel that was wrapped around him . . .' (John 13:4-5. NIV).

This was something new to me. Here before me was displayed an example of humility and of service, which I would never forget, and it struck at the root of my pride. As I did the work I was asked to do I kept before me the perfect example of Jesus, who became a servant for me: then it was not too difficult to serve others for him.

I was in that house for five weeks before my baptism. When I asked the Rev Aslam Khan about the delay, he said,

'Oh, I have arrangements to make.' I realised later that he wanted to observe me for a while, to make sure that I was serious about being baptised. It wouldn't have been good to take this step and then go back from it.

But I grew agitated for fear of discovery. I wondered if my family were making enquiries yet of Razia, so I wrote to her:

'I still have some business to transact here, before I return. Please do not tell my family where I am. I will explain everything to you soon.'

I later learned that Razia and her mother were as good as their word, and managed to keep my secret, though it brought them a great deal of trouble. I am glad to say she is married now - a faithful, honest friend who defended me then at great cost, though not understanding the moves I was making.

All the time I was with Mr and Mrs Khan I was attending the Methodist Church on Warris Road. Among Christian people I found a freedom I had never known before in worship. There were many things that were different here.

The first thing that I noticed when I walked in was the decoration. In the Islamic mosque the decoration is purely abstract – words from the Quran, patterns on tiles, columns, domes, carpets. Light and shade are used too for effect. Never is the human figure portrayed nor any picture of God, for how can the created thing imagine its creator? Here there was coloured glass in the windows, with a picture of Jesus praying, there were flowers on a table, and music. Over the arch were, not words in Arabic but the words, 'Behold I stand at the door and knock.' I thought about that. In Pakistan there is a lot of knocking. Everyone bangs hard on doors and gates, but the knocking of Jesus on my heart's door was so gentle.

The next thing I noticed was the lovely way in which families sat together – men, women and children. Single people were drawn in to these family groups. At home usually only the men would go to the mosque. The women said their prayers at home. I realised how little teaching many of them received, but then the Quran says that women are inferior to men, though it also stresses they should be treated with justice and equality. But the men represent their women in the mosque. How different it is in Christianity, where God deals with each soul through Jesus, who died for each one.

The Bible says that in Christ there are no differences of race (Jew nor Greek), class (bond nor free) or sex (male nor female). Here was equal treatment of a new and wondrous kind. God received my worship equally with that of my brothers in Christ, and the fellowship of believers was expressed in meeting together as the Body of Christ.

I sensed these invisible cords binding that whole church together in this new 'Christian fellowship' in the prayers that they prayed for the sick and the old and those in trouble. I felt it as they welcomed me into their midst. Gradually I began to feel as if the church was taking the place of the family I had left behind. Here I had brothers and sisters in plenty.

I noticed that the minister's preaching was along simple lines, but it dealt with profound things, from a book that made sense to me. Through his teaching I heard the Lord Jesus speaking, not quite as directly as he had to me in my room, but in a way which applied the Bible to my life.

Yet I also noticed that he spoke as if he were trying to convince some of his hearers. I began to realise that some people who called themselves 'Christians' were not as whole-hearted as I was. I had lived in a strictly orthodox environment since birth, and had probably not realised that this would be true of Muslims also.

My host had warned me about telling people too much about myself. I did however tell a little about my healing and my conversion and the people at church were amazed.

'Do you mean that Jesus appeared to you in your room and healed you?'

I wondered why my experience was so rare. Surely Jesus could work as he had for me in every believer's life?

'It is according to your faith,' said Aba-ji when I asked him. This was a liberating statement. I saw there was a principle involved here – that faith was the key to the continuance of this wondrous Christian experience and life of miracle on which I had embarked. I thought back and saw how my faith had grown almost unsuspected by me, from the failure to find healing at Mecca. It had come as a gift, this faith that moved mountains. It had grown out of helplessness and need. My cry had risen to the ear of a God I did not know, but who knew me, and He had moved in on my life. I determined, in the night's quiet, to keep my faith strong, no matter what obstacles lay ahead.

At last the day of my baptism came, April 23rd. This took place in a room in the house in which there was a tank for this kind of event. The Major and his wife and some of their friends and mine gathered. The minister of Warris Road performed the ceremony, which was simple and perfect. As he immersed me in the tank I felt I was leaving the old Gulshan down there on the bottom, with her old ways of thinking and her old desires and a new Gulshan was emerging, 'buried with him in baptism and raised to newness of life.'

That new life surged through me and I longed to witness to it. Those elders who were present gave me a new name: Gulshan Esther. I read later that Esther was a witness to the King about God's people the Jews, and she was in danger. It seemed to me very appropriate in my case.

After the service the women came and kissed me on the forehead and the men shook my hand as they welcomed me to the church of Christ. I felt warmed by their true Christian love. When they had gone Mr Aslam Khan asked me how I felt.

'Fine,' I answered. 'But now I want to witness to what has happened.'

He shook his head. 'You can witness by your actions. It's not necessary to witness only by your mouth.'

But I remembered the words Jesus had spoken to me: 'You are my witness. Go to my people.'

I looked at him, head up, refusing to be beaten.

'But I feel that Jesus wants me to witness. Can I speak in the church?'

'I don't think you are really ready for that. You have a witness in the home to fulfil. God will accept that.'

But he didn't know this Gulshan Esther. I said: 'Well, if I can't witness here then I must go home and tell my family. I want to do that in any case.'

He looked really worried at that. 'No, it would be dangerous for you. They wouldn't like your baptism at all and they may harm you.'

'I don't believe my family would do anything to harm me, but I won't go until it seems right. Will you instead send me to Bible college so that I might learn more to tell them?'

He looked down at me steadily and I wondered what he was thinking. I began to feel a little embarrassed by my forwardness in pushing so hard for my own way. I was young and eager to do the work I was sure God had set before me, but I did not realise then how inexperienced and raw I was. I had only just begun the real pilgrimage of my life.

'I don't think we can do this just yet.' Mr Aslam Khan spoke firmly. 'You're too young in the faith, but if you must find some piece of Christian work to do we can get you into the Sunrise School for the Blind.'

He explained to me a little about the School, and how it cared for blind children who could not be educated in the normal system. He thought he could get me a job there as a housemother. I agreed to this, excited at the thought.

I had already met the principal of the School, so the arrangements were quickly made for him to come and fetch me in his van. As, next day, we drove over the Old Ravi Bridge, and its dirty bit of river, and into the square compound of Sunrise School, I felt that I was cutting myself loose from my past life. From now onwards I was a new person, with a new name and a new destiny.

My time as a housemother at Sunrise School for the Blind, Lahore, marked a new stage of growth. From being dependent on others, at one stroke I became responsible for a group of little blind children, having to care for their physical needs. In a completely new world I had to learn to cope, to stand on my own feet. It was not easy.

Not easy, but better than it might have been. This solid red-brick building had seen many changes since it was founded by its Indian benefactor Sir Ganga Ram, as a hospital or leprosarium. His ashes lay next door in a perfectly deplorable *samedhi*. Miss Fyson took over the institute in 1958 as a Christian School for the Blind, retiring in 1969. I thought of her gratefully. For me it was a perfect, protected environment for learning to live in the world outside the veil. As a mark of my breakaway from my old life I cut my hair short, and had the tailor make me two white coats to wear over my *shalwar kameeze* when out.

To my delight I found that here were real rewards – not in rupees, for the pay was only about 40 a month – but in the uncritical love of my young charges. The children in the School ranged in age from five to 16. Half were Muslims and half Christians and the two worked and played very happily together, the only separation being for religious teaching and prayer. There were 40 children in my section of the School. I was to look after the younger boys, be with them at meals, be their eyes in the grounds of the School, and sleep in their dormitory. I was to care for their clothes and some of the washing, help them to wash themselves, make their beds, and supervise a task they did not do well – washing their dishes after meals. I also had to clean the windows and scrub the tables.

In addition I was to teach the children the Bible and once a fortnight it would be my turn to take them to church.

There were two other housemothers, cousins, who were Christians. At first they were unfriendly, speaking to each other but not to me, though we worked closely together, and showing their dislike in other inconvenient ways. But after a few days they warmed to me and began to help me with the work that I found difficult, and be my interpreter to the principal who spoke only English, not Urdu.

94

Now when they had to go for paste and soap to the principal's office, they asked for me too. They helped me when I was in trouble with my hands. The work was rougher than I had been used to, and my hands were tender. In the first week they became very chapped from the soap we used for washing clothes. Then I scalded one hand while in the kitchen. Finally, while scrubbing tables I got splinters in my hands and they bled. I was in a great deal of discomfort. Rosina, one of the cousins, came with me to the principal to translate for me.

He was very sympathetic, but as he gave the ointment to Rosina for the scald he told me:

'There is nothing I can do to relieve you of this work. I am sorry, but if you cannot do it you might have to leave. See if the others can help you.'

'Don't worry, we'll help you,' said Rosina comfortingly as we went back to our quarters, and I smiled gratefully at her.

Back in my room I took my troubles to my never-failing source of comfort. I soon saw that whereas my hands were only scalded – perhaps by my own carelessness – Christ's hands were nailed to a cross for me, and my sufferings were as nothing compared to that.

Underneath the surface, however, more serious battles were about to be fought.

Soon after I arrived at Sunrise I phoned my younger brother, Alim Shah. I told him:

'I thought you should know that I have become a Christian in earnest, and now I am working at a School for blind children in Lahore.'

There was a gasp at the other end of the line: 'What is this that you have done?' said Alim Shah. 'Come, return home and forget all about this.'

'Now that I have found the way, the truth and the life, how can I forget all about it?'

He said: 'Have you gone quite mad? If you keep on saying this to me my door will be shut to you for ever. As far as I am concerned you are dead.'

'All right, you tell me this: how can I leave the truth and come back to you? I cannot do this at any cost.'

His tone was grim and even: 'I see. In that case my door is shut. You are dead! I never want to see your face again and you will never see mine.'

I smiled at that. 'All right. If your door is shut my heavenly Father's door is open to me. If I'm dead as far as you're concerned it's because I'm dead in Jesus Christ. And if you also die in Jesus Christ, then you also will live – and then you'll see me.'

His answer was to bang down the phone.

On the same day I wrote to my uncle telling him that I'd become a Christian, and had been baptised. I also wrote to Safdar Shah, saying the same thing. I waited to see what their reaction would be, with nervous anticipation, longing for them to understand, to accept me as I was now and allow me to live amongst them again. But in my heart of hearts I knew that this might not be possible. They would never allow me freedom to worship as I pleased, if I went home.

During this time I confided in no one at the School. This was on the Rev Aslam Khan's advice. I was in a precarious position, with so much opposition building up, and the kindly minister really feared for me, and for other Christians involved with me. So when the children asked me about myself I avoided giving direct answers. But I had many other things to tell them that they wanted to hear. They loved to listen when I told them stories from the Bible.

'Oh *Baji*,' the cry would go up at bedtime. 'Please tell us another story.'

'Well, just one more and then it's lights out.' And I would read them or tell them stories that Jesus told, about the ninety-nine sheep that were safely in their pen and about the one that was out on the hills alone, lost. I told them about the younger son who got all the money his father was going to leave him and went away and wasted it all, so that no one wanted him as a friend and no father would trust him with his daughter's dowry. I also told them the stories that came into the Quran – about Abraham and Isaac and Ishmael and Sara and Hagar. Muslims believe that Abraham (whom they call Ibrahim) prepared to offer Ishmael in sacrifice. The Bible account says that Abraham offered Isaac, who was the legitimate son.

There were rules in the home against giving religious 'colour' when telling the stories to Muslims, so I would work within these rules. I told the children both versions and then I would ask, 'Which one is the truth?'

Each group would say their own was right. At least they got to know from me that there were two versions.

We sang songs together. I taught them hymns and choruses, which all the children loved. A great favourite, which was sung with great gusto, was:

'Sing them over again to me,
Wonderful words of life.
Let me more of their beauty see,
Wonderful words of life.'

After 9 pm roughly our day was over and then I found time to read and study the Bible for myself. Each time I came to open it I found the same thing happening. It was as if I had an interpreter, helping me to understand. If I asked myself one night, 'What does this mean?' I could be sure that before many days had passed I understood. I was growing in spiritual awareness!

This kind of learning was matched by what I gained from the blind children. They met all their handicaps with patience and cheerfulness. I loved them for it, and watching them, learned also. Perhaps I understood their situation so well since I felt, as I watched them at play, that I too had been blind once to God's love. Now I could see.

Then my family counter-attacked. I received a letter from Safdar Shah. I had been waiting for it, with a feeling of dread.

97

He began politely, as always, by saying that he never expected to hear such news from me: 'You are my dear sister. You used to love God very much, and my father used to love you very much and you learned a lot from him about Islam. I don't really need to tell you this – you know it. You must also know that a daughter of a Sayed cannot go the way you are going. You must turn back.

'My brother has told me about your becoming a Christian, and believing in Jesus as God's Son. This is not right for our family or our religion. I suggest that as soon as you read this letter you come back to my house and listen to my advice. As you know I have the deeds to all the property which is in your name. It cannot be given to a Christian who has been the daughter of a Sayed.'

He added that the whole of Pakistan knew that I was now a Christian and was therefore not entitled to this property. The letter concluded:

'If you do not leave Christianity I will leave no stone unturned to get you back. My religion allows me to kill a sister who has become a Christian – and still go into Paradise.'

This letter upset me very much. My father had left me his property with great love and now they were seeking to deprive me of it because I had become a Christian. I thought of my white-walled bungalow and felt like crying. It did not seem fair.

But in praying over the situation I came across John 14: 1-4. 'Let not your heart be troubled. Ye believe in God, believe also in me. I go to prepare a place for you. In my Father's house are many mansions. If it were not so I would have told you.'

These words brought me comfort. I had a home promised above.

I tore up the letter and threw the pieces in the waste paper basket. Then I went to assembly and found myself singing, thinking about the words, 'What a friend we have in Jesus.'

Three days later came the third attack – a letter from my uncle at home. It was ten pages long, written on white padded paper in a blue envelope.

In it he said they were missing me very much, mentioning Salima and Sema – 'Who are they going to serve now?' That gave me a pang or two.

The letter asked me to come back home in very loving terms, and it ended:

'Have you become atheist? We are praying that you will come back to Islam and to your home.'

The sun shone on the children as they played on the grass in the middle of the compound, but where I stood with the letter in my hand a grey shadow of fear and doubt laid its clammy hand on me.

I folded up the letter, praying as I did so: 'Oh Lord Jesus, I haven't done anything wrong to them. Why are they behaving like this? Now I am really surrounded by them. Will you tell me what answer to give?'

When I had time to think about it again quite a different aspect presented itself to me. They were not going to give me my property, so at least I was free from all the burden of it. I could spend my life serving in the school for the blind and going to church and worshipping.

'Isn't that better than the useless life I lived, paralysed on my bed?' I said to myself.

I spent a day thinking and praying about my answer and when I replied it was on a scrappy piece of paper from an exercise book:

'Dear Uncle,

I have received your letter and I am aware of all that you have said. With the greatest respect I would like to point out five things:
1. I have found the way, which is the straight path to God. Jesus said 'I am the door. By me if any man enter in he shall be saved and shall go in and out and find pasture' (John 10:9). If you go to any house you cannot enter but by

the door. There is a door to God and that door is Jesus. Those who do not accept Christ's way cannot knock on the door. The prophets are *chowkedars*.

2. I have found the truth. 'Because I tell you the truth you do not believe me. Which of you convinceth me of sin?' (John 8:45).

3. I have found the life. Jesus said 'I am the resurrection and the life. He that believes in me, though he die yet shall he live' (John 11:25).

4. I have found forgiveness of sin.

5. I have found everlasting life. 'For God so loved the world that he gave his only begotten son that whosoever believeth in him should not perish but have everlasting life' (John 3:16). You have called me an atheist; come and prove it through these five things that I have found. Either you prove it or take a warning from me not to call me an atheist.'

I said nothing about property or about any other issue. From that day to this I have never had an answer to this letter.

After this, for several months I was left in peace, but Uncle and Aunty, a few weeks after receiving my reply, I later learned, packed up their belongings, said they were going to Karachi and fled the house, some say to Iran, since they were Shia Muslims. This was because they feared the wrath of Safdar Shah, who was holding them responsible for what had happened.

10: Sisters

December came – and with it the preparations for Christmas. Most of the blind children would be going to their homes, but some were staying. So we decorated the dining room with a tree and some streamers, and made a little manger, and saw the light of wonder at the simple story of the Christ child's coming dawn on happy, excited faces.

For me too it was an experience – my first taste of this Christian feast. As I have sung so often since then,

'How silently, how silently the wondrous gift is given,
So God imparts to human hearts the blessings of His heaven.'

It is no wonder that even nominal Christians, who have never been introduced to the Founder of their faith, find blessing in celebrating his birth, whether in turkey and plum pudding or chicken, pilau and sweet rice. The joy of Christmas crosses all boundaries.

The principal and his wife gave each child little presents of sweets and small toys, and we all went to service at the Salvation Army in the Sunrise van. We housemothers were invited to their bungalow for an evening.

Soon after Christmas, I received an unexpected visitor, bringing terrible news. My brother-in-law, Blund Shah from Rawalpindi, came to the School to see me. He stood in the visitors' room, looking tired and crushed, and told me that my sister, Anis, was seriously ill in Gujerat, where she had been for the last three months, in a rented bungalow, having treatment during a difficult pregnancy from her family doctor who had moved there to a hospital. In the seventh month the pregnancy had gone wrong. The baby was dead and the doctors from the hospital could not stop the bleeding.

'She is at the point of death and keeps repeating your name. Would you come straight away with me now? I have the car outside.'

It was a summons I could not refuse. A door I thought shut for ever stood ajar.

'Oh, my poor sister! Of course I will come, but first I must ask permission.'

I excused myself and left the room. A tiny whisper in my ear said: 'She will be dead when you arrive. It is a waste of time going. They will not let you speak of these things. They might even try to prevent your return.'

Before seeing the principal I went to my room and prayed. The answer came clearly: 'You go down to her. She will not die. I will keep her alive.'

I asked for two days' leave, was given it, and threw some small things in my bag. We left at 5 pm. A three hour journey brought us to the house in Gujerat, where we were greeted with dreadful news.

'She is dead,' said my sister's doctor, Mrs Khan. 'She died at 7 o'clock. She has lost too much blood.'

I went into the room where my sister lay. She had a yellow-grey, pinched look, and her lips were blue. My sister's husband gave way to a rush of tears and was guided sympathetically out of the room by one of his family.

The room filled up with mourners . . . members of the family and neighbours – the news of a death travels fast and people come quickly to pay their respects to the dead one.

I knelt down and wept beside the bed. 'Jesus,' I said in my heart. 'You told me she would be alive. What shall I do? She is dead.'

I continued to pray. 'Jesus, You are the way, the truth and the life. Please do this miracle and raise her up.' I kept on praying this, until the thought came to me powerfully that Jesus had said, 'She will not die. I will keep her alive.' So I prayed: 'Lord, you put some life in her so that I can talk to her for a while about you.' Then at length I heard a voice, 'She is not dead. She is alive. I have added to her life.'

I got up at this and told everyone. 'Why are you all crying? She is not dead – she is alive.'

There was general consternation. 'She is mad. Put her in the other room. Lock her up.'

They thrust me out, and into an empty bedroom. I heard the latch click down on the outside. I was effectively a prisoner. I prayed on: 'Lord, wake up my sister so that they can believe she is alive.'

By now they were carrying out the last offices and preparing the coffin. My sister's body had been washed and her clothes changed earlier. She would be bathed again, but not at night. So it was about 8 am before the outside latch clicked once more and I was released to pay my last respects to my sister.

I was standing by her bed with other ladies. The *maulvi's* wife said the *Kalmas* over the body and then she and three others moved forward to pick up the body to give it its final bath. I saw on her hands and feet the red henna . . . the sign of happiness, the sign of blood. . . . They would afterwards wrap my sister in a sheet and put her in the box.

Suddenly my sister moved her arm, opened her eyes, sat bolt upright and looked around her in wonder. Then she studied her hands vaguely and asked, 'What happened?'

People screamed, fell backwards, some tried to escape from the room. There was unbelievable panic. I embraced Anis and she clung to me. The people came back. Then they all looked at me. 'What have you done? How can a dead person sit up?'

I was filled with joy, and with a sense of the greatness of God. I said, smiling: 'Ask her what happened.'

Anis spoke then in her usual calm manner. 'Don't be frightened of me. I am alive.'

Her husband and the imam, maulvi and muezzin from the mosque came running in, hearing the commotion. The maulvi put his hand on her head and asked, '*Beiti*, tell me

103

the truth. What happened? What happened to you? Fourteen hours ago you died. We were preparing for your funeral!'

She said, 'I was not dead.'

The lady doctor was there. 'You were dead. There was no life in you,' she insisted.

'I was not dead, I was sleeping,' said my sister. 'In my sleep I had a dream that I was about to put my foot on a ladder. At the top of the ladder there was a man in a white robe who was wearing a golden crown, and there was a light coming out from his forehead. I saw his hand above me and there was a light coming from his hand. He said: "I am Jesus Christ, King of Kings. I will send you back, and at the appointed time I will bring you here again." And then I opened my eyes.'

She said this with a face alight with joy. Words could not describe the joy and rejoicing in our family. I took the opportunity of telling any who would listen about the miracle-working prophet, who was more than a prophet – Jesus.

Even Anis's husband, who had been one of those most against me in the beginning, now said that my prayers had brought his wife back to life.

'Who is this great prophet you have seen?' he asked, after three days when the guests had dispersed. I took the Quran and showed him the passages about Jesus in the Sura Maryam. Then I showed him in my Bible the story of the raising of Lazarus in John 11:43-44: 'Now do you believe that Jesus raises the dead? It says here that he called "Lazarus, come out," and he came.'

Slowly he replied, 'Yes, I believe this is from Jesus, Son of Mary. My wife has a second life.' He seemed quite happy and accepting what I told him.

It was in Anis herself that the greatest change took place. She was always a loving sister to me, but now she seemed to radiate joy and peace. I heard her telling the *maulvi* and his wife all about her vision of Jesus, and I noted that they listened with intense concentration. But after that they started to eye me with disfavour.

'Tell me more about Jesus,' she whispered in one of the brief times we were able to be alone. So I gave her a small copy of the New Testament and she promised to read it, though she felt she needed someone to help her understand it. She started with Matthew's Gospel and I explained how Jesus was born, and what was his pedigree.

'Keep praying for me. I shall remain faithful to what I have seen so that I can follow him who gave me life,' she said. 'I am married, so I need some prayer.'

My eyes filled with tears. I felt her position keenly.

With all these happenings I had pushed Sunrise to the back of my mind, but suddenly I realised that I should get back. In truth I was eager to go and tell someone of these miracles. When I left, to get the bus back to Lahore, Anis squeezed my hand and said: 'My door is open to you. Whenever you like you can come back. Even if the rest of the family do not want to see you, I do.'

As the bus pulled out of Gujerat bus station, laden with people from both country and town, I settled down to think through the events of the visit, now disappearing like a happy dream behind me. It had underlined one thing – I loved those people and their world still, but I could no longer live in it. I was a pilgrim, not on the road to Mecca, but on a more direct route to God, through Jesus. Sunrise had become part of my pilgrim's way. As the bus lurched along the road to Lahore I looked forward to greeting my blind boys again.

But all unaware I had committed a grievous error. The authorities at the school said so when I appeared some time later, now three days overdue.

'You asked for two days and you have taken five.'

It was a painful interview, and I got the sack, without really having a chance to explain myself. I committed my defence to God and left Him to be the judge.

A few minutes later I stood at the side of the Ravi Road by an electric light pole, still shocked and bewildered by the suddenness of my eviction. I was hungry – it was past

lunch time and I had eaten nothing since an early breakfast. It was cold and cloudy. It would get dark early
today. I remembered that the dhobi had some of my
clothes and my bedding, which had not been returned to
me. The blind, patient faces of small boys came before
me, and tears stung my eyes. They would have no more
stories from their *Ba-ji*. And I was also owed money. I
had none except for some my sister had given me that
morning. I stood there perplexed, aware that it was a lonely
area, and that a Muslim convert could expect little protection.

'Father,' I said to God, surrendering my fate into his
hands, 'There are good and bad people in this city. Have
you any room for your daughter? Please tell me where I
should go.'

Immediately I knew the answer: 'Go back to Gujerat.'

I had enough for the fare. I caught the 2 pm bus and
then a tonga and surprised my sister. She threw her arms
about me and said happily:

'I am so glad you have come back to me. Now you will
help me to understand the Bible.'

Even Blund Shah was pleased to see me back, since I
would be a companion to his wife. She was missing her
children, two daughters of eight and six who were in
Rawalpindi with their grandparents. He too had to be there
to check on his bus business in which he was a partner.

So for a time my sister and I enjoyed a new relationship,
without hindrance. Like two young lambs we grazed on the
green pastures of the words of God, and my sister visibly
altered as she learned more about the experience of new
life. She was less bossy to the servants and would sometimes do the work herself. She would even ask the servants
to eat first, saying, 'The poor have the first right.' She had
found the verse 'Esteem others better than yourself.'

When I asked, just to make sure of her motives, 'Why
are you doing this?' she replied, 'So that if I die tomorrow I
will know where I stand, because I am trying to be one of
His obedient servants.'

The maids' reaction was one of real surprise. 'Since our Bibi has come back from the dead she has become like an angel,' they told me. They worked harder than ever for her, serving her from the heart. To me they showed great respect.

One day she questioned me about my baptism, and listened carefully to my explanation of its meaning. I told her, 'It is important that you be buried with Christ in baptism if you really want life. When we are baptised we are cleansed in body, mind and soul and we become his people.'

Then she said; 'I want to be baptised, since I am a Christian now. I have changed in my heart and I want to go a step further.'

My delight was mingled with alarm. It had cost me a great deal to be baptised. Did she really understand what price she would have to pay for this act?

But Anis insisted. 'It will hurt me if I am not baptised,' she said. 'I will not be a Muslim and I will not be a Christian. I will be outside,' she told me firmly, and I capitulated. What right had I to refuse to help her? But I saw at once that I could not seek the aid of a Christian minister – that would be to invite disaster from Blund Shah's family, if from no one else. I would have to perform the ceremony myself.

One afternoon we asked the maid to fill the deep cemented tub with tepid water and lay out some towels and clean clothes. Then we dismissed her. I saw her curious dark eyes linger on us as we closed the bathroom door.

I stood with Anis in the water and asked her if she would confess to belief in Christ. She said, 'Now I bury my old self and am new in Jesus, and I shall be faithful.'

Then I immersed her in the name of the Father, Son and Holy Ghost, and committed her to God's keeping. It was a moment of triumph. Afterwards Anis told me that when she prayed she was lifted up as if on angels' wings and saw in a vision people standing around and glorifying Jesus.

I was beginning to learn, however, that whenever I felt joy over something I had to beware and watch for the activity of dark forces of evil, and this occasion was no exception. My brother-in-law heard about the baptism. I think that sharp-eared maid had told him something and he questioned my sister about what we had been doing.

Anis looked scared, 'He asked me about it last night, and I told him what the baptism meant. Now he is angry. He does not like or understand all this about the cross. I cannot explain it. I think he is looking for a chance to have an argument with you. Please try not to upset him, or he will make you go.'

I tried to be especially agreeable to my brother-in-law, but eventually I tumbled into an argument with him.

He challenged me to tell him the difference between reading the Quran and reading the Bible. Of course I had to tell him that Jesus made the difference. He was the way, the truth and the life. . .

'Reading the Bible is all right, but the cross is not all right,' said Blund Shah. 'It says even in your Bible that only a man who is cursed will die on the cross and how can a man who is cursed give life to others.' He wore a triumphant look. He thought me trapped.

This was just the opening I needed. I read him 1 Corinthians 1:18 – 'For the message of the cross is foolishness to them that believe not.'

He said nothing, so emboldened I read him John 1:29 – 'Behold the lamb of God that taketh away the sin of the world.'

My sister sat listening, a faraway look in her eyes, not interfering.

I took him to the Torah, to his Muslim roots, and I explained how blood sacrifices for substitution were given by God to Abraham, but after Jesus there was no need for them any more. I showed him this from Genesis 22:11-12 'Do not lay your hand on the boy,' and then from John 12:32 – 'I, if I be lifted up from the earth, will draw all men to me.' I told him that it was by the great sacrifice of Jesus on the cross that our sins were forgiven . . . the perfect and complete substitute.

I told him that I found mention of these things in the Quran first and then found fuller understanding in the Bible. I told him about the prophets who predicted the coming of Jesus. I told him also that the Bible was not just a book but the living word of God, and that whatever happened in my life I found help for it in the Bible.

I finished with Acts 4:11-12: 'The stone that the builders rejected is made head of the corner. Neither is there salvation in any other, for there is no other name under heaven, given among men, whereby we must be saved.'

All this was at 10 am in the morning living room. He sat there, as if mesmerised. Then he recovered, and looked at me narrowly. 'Do you want to make me a Christian too? You are staying here and eating from my table and undermining our Muslim beliefs in this way! Get out, now, and this time don't come back.'

My sister smuggled some money to me and whispered, 'Don't go back to Lahore. Go to Rawalpindi and I will find you there when I come.'

She gave me the address of an important family friend, another Shia, whose husband was a high ranking government official. She held high positions in charitable societies concerned to improve the lot of women, giving them better conditions. She might have some work for me.

This was good news. I had to get a job. So I went back to the bus station by tonga and caught a bus to Rawalpindi. Three and a half hours later I climbed into another tonga, which dropped me at the gate of the imposing residence on the Peshawar Road. I sent in a note bearing my name and my father's name, so that the lady I sought would know I was a close family friend, and would remember who I was.

Invited in, I went through the high gate in the wall, feeling that this was a right step and trusting for a good outcome.

11: Trapped

I stood in the drawing room of the lady I had come to see, bearing her scrutiny as well as I could. She was a distinguished looking woman, taller than I, with a fair complexion and short hair. She wore a pink *shalwar kameeze* and a sweater, with a black embroidered shawl wrapped around her shoulders.

She smiled at me affectionately. 'How nice of you to come to see me. I don't think we have met before? My husband is not here though. He is in Islamabad until tonight. He is a very busy man.'

I murmured that I had heard he was a very important man. The lady inclined her graceful head and called for tea to be served to us. While it was drunk from fine flower-patterned china cups, she kept up a remarkable flow of polite conversation, asking after my health, and how I had travelled from Gujerat. She was very concerned to hear about Anis. I did not go into details sensing she would not want the maids to hear what I had to say.

When we had finished our tea she invited me to follow her. She led me to her bedroom, closed the door, asked me to sit, then turned to ask the questions which had hung in the air, unspoken between us:

'Why have you come without a veil? And why alone? In your family girls don't come out like this. What happened to you? Are you in any trouble?'

I was wearing a white coat with the *shalwar kameeze* and I had a scarf wound round my head. I had long ago given up wearing the *burka*. However, I had no wish to argue about that just now.

I said, 'You are surprised to see me without the veil.

Doesn't it surprise you to see me walking? You know I was a cripple and sick in bed for nineteen years?'

'I know that. But now tell me, which doctor treated you to make you so well?'

'I will show you my doctor.' I read to her the story of the cripple who was carried by four people and raised by Jesus in Mark 2:9-11, then I handed her the Urdu Bible to see for herself.

She took the book as if it were a snake, looked at it for a moment and then handed it back. 'This book belongs to Christians,' she said with an expression of disgust.

'That is right, and I also am a Christian,' I replied.

She gripped the arm of her chair. 'What am I hearing?'

'This is the truth. The person who has healed me, I belong to him now.'

'What exactly do you mean by that?' So I told her the story, leaving out names of Christians.

My hostess was making an effort to compose herself. She rose from her chair and took a few quick paces around the room, then came to sit down opposite me again and, leaning forward, fixed me with a look of intense concern.

'But then,' she said, 'if Jesus heals you, is it a necessity to become a Christian?'

'In my case, yes. I have found a new life, and now I belong to the person who has given me a new life. For his sake I have been thrown out of my house. But I haven't come here to discuss religion with you. I have come here to ask you if you would get me some job in one of your women's institutions. Can you do this? A simple job will do; I am not expecting a highly-paid one.'

There was a short silence, while she studied the pattern on the rich carpet. 'I see. Do you know I really thought that someone had kidnapped you from your home and that you had found your way here to ask for help.'

She laughed mirthlessly. 'All right. You shall stay here with me for one night, and then tomorrow I will arrange something for you.'

She gave me a room to myself, and I was served with supper by one of her maids. I said a short prayer and went to bed, tired but at rest. Family ties, even at this distance were, after all, stronger than I had thought.

Next morning after breakfast, which I took alone in the dining room, I met her husband. He took the offensive immediately, asking me, courteously, to renounce Christianity. Of course I declined his request, equally courteously. I was shivering inside because here was a powerful man in the government. It would be easy for him to brush me away like an annoying mosquito, even though I was a close family friend.

He said, 'Think about what you are saying. There is still time for you to embrace Islam again, and I will help you to be reconciled with your family.' Was there an implied threat there? I took a fresh hold on my nerves. I had an opportunity here that must not be lost.

'Thank you, but no,' I said. 'I have not quarrelled with them. I am at peace with everyone. The one in whom I believe is the Prince of Peace, and he can give you peace too.' The words came out before I knew I had said them.

'Why don't you leave Christianity?' he said, losing a little of his glacial patience. 'If you don't want to stay with your brother or your sister, stay with me for the rest of your life.'

It was a most handsome offer, and no doubt sincerely meant.

'Thank you, but my Christianity is not just a religion, which one can give up when one feels like it, it is a change of life. If I give up living in Christ I would die.'

Then I added, 'Look, if you cannot arrange some work for me, tell me and then I will go and not bother you again.'

For a moment he stood like a statue, then he turned away. 'Oh yes, we will arrange something for you.' He winked at his wife as he went out of the door.

I heard her call to her driver to get the car ready. 'Come,' she said and we got into the car and were driven into the city. The car stopped outside a large iron gate, set in high walls. Beyond I could see the top of a large cement building. A sign announced that it was the Central Jail, Rawalpindi. So this was where I was to work.

The driver called to the guard, who opened the gate. My friend took me inside to the office of the superintendent and she talked with him for a few moments in English, quite obviously about me. The superintendent then rang a bell, and an elderly woman appeared, jangling a bunch of keys. The superintendent said something I could not hear and nodded in my direction and the woman said to me, 'Come.'

My kind friend said, 'You go with this lady. This place will be better for you.'

I thanked her warmly and followed the woman out across a verandah. A barred gate was unlocked and the woman showed me into a long room, like a hall, with a high ceiling, and no windows. Such light as there was came from a barred gate set in one of the walls. There was another, solid gate on the opposite wall. About ten women squatted on dirty mats of woven palm leaves, or hessian, or leaned against the walls in attitudes of sullen indifference. I heard the door bang shut behind me, and a key turn in the lock, and I looked helplessly at the nearest woman.

'What is happening? Where is the job I am to do?'

'Job? There is no job here. You are in prison, like us. What have you done to be in here?'

It took a minute or two to sink in. This so-called family friend had sent me to prison for the offence of being a Christian! I had been tricked and trapped. I ran to the gate and shook the bars. No one came. I called out. No one answered, except the young woman who had spoken before.

'You can shout all you like – it won't get you out.'

I turned to her: 'What is this place?'

'You should know, oh green one. This is the remand prison, where they keep you till trial, or you can get someone to bail you.' It was all expressed in somewhat stronger terms than that.

I tried to remain calm and think. How long would I be kept here? What crime would they charge me with? Was being a Christian a crime? Surely by the constitution being a member of a minority was not a crime. However, by Islamic law, I was guilty of the gravest offence, and had become like an untouchable to my family.

That thought reminded me of Anis's promise to find me. Surely she would come soon. Then my eye fell on my bag. By some mercy they had not taken it from me. And my Bible was in it, with some fresh clothes – treasures beyond compare in that place.

I looked around me more carefully. Where could I rest in this place? The room was about 80 feet in length, with three or four side rooms in which were iron-framed beds, covered by dark blankets. These were out of the draughts of Himalayan night air which came from the barred gate. But one glance told me I could not sleep there. The rooms were very dark and airless, with no windows – like tombs. And I had no wish to be eaten alive by the inhabitants of those blankets. Out on the cold, hard, dirty floor the other women wrapped themselves totally in sheets and lay down on the dirty mats. Wrapped in as many garments as I could put on I sat up all night, looking drowsily beyond prison bars to the clean night sky, with its moon and stars.

Hygiene was a problem which continually vexed me, as it did the other women. A very unpleasant odour in the room advertised the presence of a toilet but there was no running water and no proper washing facilities – just one *mutka* or pitcherful between us to last all day, for both washing and drinking. This was filled each morning by the waterman. There was a cup on a chain attached to the top of the pitcher, two glasses for drinking from, and a *lotha* for ritual ablutions. I never noticed anyone use it for that purpose during the time I was there. Prayer was very far from their minds.

Three times a day a jailer brought something resembling food – dry bread and tea for breakfast, and for other meals, thin lentil soup, undercooked chapatties and occasionally tasteless egg-plant. The sight of these provisions – which I would not have fed to the beggars at home – caused the

114

prisoners to fly into such a rage they would sometimes throw the tea over the jailer and fall to cursing him, and the cook, and the police and the courts and each other with language that made me stop my ears.

Beyond the barred gate we could see, in the distance, at intervals, family members or friends of the prisoners, bringing comforts. Then the gate would swing open and one or two of the women would be taken out to a visitors' room for a short time, returning with supplies to make life bearable – clean sheets, food. Soon sweet rice and pilau and pieces of chicken were going around, but none came my way.

No one showed any interest in my presence, or any desire to charge me with any offence. Yet, I learned, this was meant to be a temporary prison only, for those awaiting trial. How long could one languish here without trial?

I asked the elderly woman warder, 'Why am I here?'

'I don't know why. Superintendent ordered me,' said the woman indifferently. 'I was just carrying out orders.'

From one of the other prison blocks on the male side I heard the screams of men being beaten, severely. I heard the other women – some of whom appeared to have connections with gangs in the city – say that this was to extract suitable confessions in order to make a proper charge. I learned too that it was possible for women to be beaten – by women – for the same purpose. I waited, wondering if this was to be my fate.

For the first week I could neither sleep properly on the hard floor nor eat the prison food. One sniff at the soup made me lose such appetite as I had. I did not enjoy the dirt, or the lice, the smells, or, at first, the company. Yet when tossed on waves of doubt, billows of fear, I would read some part of my precious Bible – and I found that the world gradually righted itself and peace began to flow like a river. I read about Peter and John in prison in Acts 12: 6-8. It occurred to me that it was as much a shock to them to be treated like common criminals as it was to me. But they gave thanks and sang praises. The apostle Paul too, writing from prison said: 'In everything give thanks.' All right

115

then, I would give thanks for being able to prove God in similar circumstances.

At first, as I used enforced idleness to meditate on the words of God, I tried to shut myself off from my cell-mates. Most of them, it was obvious to me, were criminals who loved evil, members of gangs and the off-scourings of the big city, shoplifters, pickpockets, kidnappers, and one murderess from North West Frontier Province, who had killed her husband. Oh that pride! This prison was to be the perfect cure for it.

My patient silence, as I addressed myself to my book, only increased their respect for me and their curiosity. I was an enigma, which had eventually to explain itself.

'What is it that you are reading with such interest?' I looked up at the speaker, a youngish woman with a ravaged face on which was written all manner of evil. 'You have been reading that book for days and paying no attention to us. It must be good. What is it about?'

'Would you really like to know what is in this book?'

'Yes. Anything to pass the time in this hell-hole,' said the woman, whose name I gathered was Kalsoum. The other women stopped their gossiping to listen to our conversation.

So I began to speak about Him to these women.

I held up the book. 'This is a mirror.'

'How is it a mirror? I think it is a book' – another woman, whom I knew as Khatoon, looked around her friends to gather support for this idea.

'Well, it is a book which is also a mirror, because in here we see ourselves as we appear to God who is the judge of all men.'

'Not a good sight,' said one of the women with a harsh laugh.

'You are right,' I said. 'This mirror shows us the things we do and calls them 'sin.' Our sins are not good in man's sight or in God's sight. Man condemns our sins, and will punish us for what we have done. But God is holy and He must condemn us even more because of our sin. Sin does not please God. It offends Him. He must punish sin by death.'

I had the full attention of these poor women, waiting for their punishment. I went on, 'You will think "Then there is no escape for us. We must suffer our punishment." But the mirror shows us God has two ways of dealing with our sin. One way leads to death, the other leads to life, and we can choose which way we will take.'

There was a restless silence, broken by Kalsoum, who asked, 'How does the mirror do all this?'

'It shows us that God himself has provided a way of forgiving us our sin. He himself calls us sinners to come to him with our sin to be forgiven. This book tells us, "Come you who are weary and heavy laden and I will give you rest"(Matthew 11:27-30).'

I was surprised at the reaction to this. They had been following the argument closely. Said one woman: 'We can't deny we are burdened with sin. That is why we are here. No one can take away what we have done.'

I explained to her the doctrine of forgiveness as outlined in 1 John 1:8-9: 'If we confess our sins he is faithful and just to forgive us our sins and to cleanse us from all unrighteousness.'

Several of them were very moved by this. Tears sparkled in their eyes. They asked me to teach them more. So it was arranged that each morning I would take a Bible study with a group of them.

Within a very short time I began to see a change come over them, which shone through the veil of dirt. It wasn't just that they shared their chicken and pilau with me, or that I had a clean sheet to wrap myself in for sleeping. The best result was that seven of them confessed their sins to God, and admitted guilt for matters they were denying to the authorities, including the murderess from North West Frontier Province, and two pickpockets. They assured me that they would never commit crimes again. 'This is the work that you came into prison to do,' I told myself as the month dragged on its weary way.

117

Three of the women were taken for trial and they went, with tears because they were leaving me. But then I too was summoned. The prison door opened and I was taken to the superintendent's sitting room, where I found a horrified Anis waiting with the friend I had trusted – the latter trying to look as unconcerned as possible.

Anis flew to me and threw her arms around me, as dirty as I was. Then she turned to the older woman and began to cross-question her:

'What has my sister done to be put in prison? Has she murdered anyone?'

'Your sister has become a Christian. She has denied Islam.' That, her tone implied, was a sin worse than murder.

'That is her own personal belief. She has found the truth and is not afraid of testifying to it, and you cannot put a person in prison for that, that is unless there are no more laws in Pakistan.'

Our friend had nothing to say to that. She shrugged her shoulders. 'Well, if you want to take her home you can.'

Anis turned to me. 'Gulshan, you must come home with me now.'

I did not relish that. 'Why should I come to your home? This prison is better than your home.'

She looked hurt. 'Why do you say that?'

'Because your husband is abusing Jesus and abusing the cross, and I do not want to hear it. Here in jail the women have been listening to me, and they have confessed Jesus and I can do some useful work.'

My sister embraced me with tears in her eyes. 'You love Jesus so much.'

'I would give my life for Jesus.' It was true. Everything that had happened had only served to strengthen me in my faith. I had been through dark tunnels of despair, but in the darkness there had been light.

Anis said, 'I also love Jesus. I want to learn more about him from you.'

She then told me what had happened to her husband.

Apparently when I left his house, that same day he was involved in an accident as a result of which he was in hospital for a month. She had not been able to contact me before, since her first duty was obviously to her husband.

She continued: 'He is not going to do anything against you now. He has given me permission to bring you home.'

How quickly are fortunes reversed. At one moment I was living with the dregs of female society in prison – and finding great sweetness in their company. A matter of an hour or so later I was soaking myself in my sister's tub in her lovely home in Satellite Town, Rawalpindi, with servants to wait on my every command – and wondering how long it would be this time before I was given my marching orders because of my inability to keep silent on the matter of my faith.

12: The tempter

I think now that that stay in Pindi with my sister and my brother-in-law was one of the happiest periods of life since becoming a Christian. Anis could not do enough for me – and her husband was kind, in a subdued way. Once more I was part of my family, and was being treated with love and consideration.

The household had servants – two or three maidservants, a clerk, a cook and a driver. The cook's son worked in the garden. No longer was I required to sew and scrub tables. It was as an entertainer of small girls that my services were now required, and I did for them what Anis once did for me – told them stories. It was an enjoyable role.

At the same time I found myself watching the maidservants with sympathetic interest, aware of all the household tasks there were to do – all the washing of dishes, floors, clothes, all the scrubbing, scouring, cleaning, polishing, dusting, all the picking up, setting out, sorting, clearing away. I found myself thanking people for their services, with a smile. It cost nothing and it spread happiness.

We drew very close together, my sister and I, sisters now in Christ. We spent two or three hours a day in study of the Bible. Very quickly Anis grasped a basic fact: it was possible to come to grips with the Bible in a way one could not with the Quran. It was in her own language, with no mystery about it. One could read it like an ordinary book, recognise from another point of view some of the events which were common to both Muslim and Jewish history, yet there was something more here, the unmistakable authority of truth.

She told me, 'These are lovely words. They bring solace.' She was thinking of her lost child.

I said, 'It is real. These are the words of our heavenly Father. Whatever you are feeling, the words for it are here, whether you are sad or happy. The main thing is to know that your sins are forgiven, and to walk with Jesus day by day.'

She said, 'I feel he is here with us, as we talk about him.'

I pointed her to the verse, 'Where two or three are gathered together in my name, there am I in the midst' (Matthew 18:20).

'When we pray he is listening. We have the Teacher with us. We understand because his Holy Spirit is guiding us.'

Blund Shah was not very happy with his wife's new interest. 'Don't you tell everybody that Christ raised you from the dead. You keep it quiet,' he told her. I don't think she took much notice of him.

For her sake I did not go out of my way to tell everybody that I was a Christian, though if they asked me directly I used to tell them of my vision and healing – that usually silenced them.

Anis and her husband had a great many relatives and friends, and every day saw its visitors to the pleasant bungalow. The conventions of a strict Shia household demanded that, whatever was happening in other parts of the Muslim world, here the fundamental divisions of the sexes remained. Male and female visitors, even if they arrived together, still sat in separate sections of the verandah, or in separate drawing rooms. There were times when I, as a Christian, felt impatient with this dividing of humanity, especially as I knew that in a society where Christ brought his people together, life could be carried along very well without them. But in Pakistan, a country founded on Islamic ideals, every part of our social life could be measured against the teachings of the Quran and their interpretation in the traditional writings. The tensions of this situation, set against city life, with its greater sophistication, were more obvious to me than they had been in

Jhang, which was rural, and backward in these matters. One part of me sat in judgement. The other part enjoyed the old relaxing pleasure of female company and female talk, unhindered by any male presence.

How soothing it was to listen to all these small details of who was to marry whom, which child was sick and which well, what they were learning at school, what careers they would follow. Girls were being educated now, some even going to college, but finding careers for them afterwards was not easy and not always desirable. A daughter might be a female doctor or a teacher of girls or a nurse. It was more difficult to go into an environment where they might work with men, as in an office. Yet keeping educated girls at home until they could be married off was becoming increasingly difficult for families, with so many young men postponing marriage while they studied for careers abroad. There was the ever-present contradiction between the religious ideal and the world as it was. Ah well, these problems faced every family nowadays – they blamed foreign influences from the West for eroding standards, and turned with relief to considerations of a happier kind – picking off the tree of dreams the richest, handsomest futures for their sons and daughters. I listened, more aware than I used to be that such dreams were fragile blossoms, ready to blow away on a rough wind. These tensions would not go away. We did not then realise how the juggling of the logic of life against the logic of religion would, repeated on a grand scale, lead to an explosion.

Anis put my thoughts into her own words. 'They are worried about the kids, but where are their lives leading?' The pointlessness of a life of religion without Christ overwhelmed her at times.

The experience of sitting on both sides of the *pardah* curtain showed me how strong and secure was the foundation I had found for my life. My happiness now was not dependant on having my personal ambitions fulfilled – it rested in doing the will of God. And so I never for one moment allowed myself to imagine that this present interlude of peace could continue for ever. And I was right.

In November I learned that my brother-in-law was going for a time from Rawalpindi to Lahore, in the interests of his bus business.

'We all have to go too,' said Anis. 'And we have to stay with Alim Shah.'

I was very dismayed at this news.

'Well, I am very sorry but I cannot come to Lahore with you. Our brother Alim Shah told me his door is shut to me since I became a Christian.'

My sister's face screwed up like a little child going to cry. 'I need your prayers and I need your help. If Alim Shah will not let you in I will rent another bungalow, and I will come with you.'

'And what would your husband do then – I think he would divorce you.' I hugged her and agreed to go with them. We would see how our brother would take my arrival.

So on November 28th we set out by car at 4 pm, and the luggage went in a truck.

'I am so pleased to see you. You are very welcome to my house.'

It was my brother Alim Shah speaking. I could not believe my ears. It was as if that bitter conversation on the phone had never happened.

The family moved in, temporarily, with Alim Shah until they found a house. I was accommodated in a nice bedroom and given a maidservant.

'I know you have your friends here,' said my brother, most unexpectedly. 'I have told my driver to take you anywhere you wish to go.'

I thanked him warmly, but underneath there was a sense of disquiet. It was all too good to be true.

When Sunday came I asked the driver to take me to Warris Road Methodist Church. The minister shook my hand at the door and the people greeted me pleasantly enough, but no one asked me, 'How are you? Where have you been? Do you need anything?' I therefore said nothing to anyone about my troubles, trusting God as always to solve them.

Four months later, one May evening I was praying in my room, sitting in a chair with the Bible open on my knees. I heard the squeak of a foot, and opened my eyes. There sat Alim Shah opposite me, watching me, with a smile on his face. I tensed, and thought of tigers for some reason.

'I hope you're happy here in my home,' he said in the kindest tone imaginable. 'I hope you're getting on with my wife and that you're happy with my children. I hope the servants don't give you any kind of trouble.'

'I'm very happy here,' I said, sincerely meaning it.

'We love you very much, and we want you to stay with us for good. In fact I'm arranging now for a bungalow to be built for you at Gulberg.' (This was a nice, modern suburb for the modestly rich, five or six miles away.)

He went on, 'And I want you to come on a holiday with me. Next month I'm going to visit Islamic countries . . . Mecca, Medina. Would you like to come with me?'

He was tempting me. I thought of 'All these things will I give you if . . .' (Matthew 4:8-9).

'I don't mind going with you,' I said, 'but it's not going to make any difference to my faith.'

As though I had not spoken he took the Bible from my lap and looked at the open pages reflectively. 'All I want from you for all that I'll give you is this book. Give me the Bible and I will take it back to the Bible Society depot so that you can't read it again. And give up going to church and I'll give you whatever you want.'

I said aloud: 'Psalm 119:105, "Your word is a lamp unto my feet and a light to my path." This is the word of God and it tells me the difference between right and wrong. I won't give it to you . . . this is a part of my life.'

I could see he was getting angry. I quickly added: 'I can't stop going to church, because it's the house of God. The Bride is getting ready and the Bridegroom is coming. "And whoever disowns me before men him will I disown before my Father which is in heaven" (Matthew 10:3).'

He jumped up. He threw the Bible at me. 'Before the sunrise, leave my home, I don't want to see you again.'

The trap had been baited. It had sprung, but it was empty. The victim had escaped.

No one else came near me that night. I lay down with a heavy heart. Next morning there was a crossness in the air. My sister-in-law didn't address one word to me. My brother was nowhere to be seen. There was no word from Anis or her husband. The servant just left the breakfast and went quietly out.

Sadly I packed my bag with four or five dresses made for me by Anis. I left my fine clothes given me by Alim Shah, because he'd said, 'Don't take anything out of this house.'

My case was in the corridor and I was going towards it, when I saw Safdar Shah coming. I hadn't seen him since I left Jhang, but the words of happy recognition died on my lips when I saw his face and what he carried. It was a gun.

He got hold of me by the wrist and pulled me downstairs to the basement of the house. 'Sit there and don't move!' he commanded me. I obeyed. Safdar Shah could, when roused, be cruel. He went to call Alim Shah. There was a deathly silence in the house, the scent of fear.

My brothers came downstairs, their faces hard and set. My heart was pounding and my legs felt like straws, but I remained seated on a sofa, trying to stay calm.

My brothers sat opposite me, on the other side of a table. I tried to look into their hate-filled eyes, but they were looking inward as if not conscious of my gaze. Safdar Shah passed the gun to Alim Shah.

'Finish this curse on the family!' he grated.

Alim Shah grasped the handle of the double-barrelled shot-gun and slowly brought it round to point at my head. He spoke with a quiet desperation:

'Why do you want to die? All you have to do is to say that you no longer accept Jesus as the Son of God, and that you will stop going to church. Your life will then be spared, for I won't shoot you.' His face looked drawn and haggard under the tube light and I saw what a terrible constraint he was under – love for me battling the love of all he had been taught by my father.

It was for me too a terrible moment. I had been brought up to treat my brothers with the greatest respect as all Muslim girls are. I had never contradicted them until Jesus came into my life, and I'd tried never to speak rudely to them, knowing that I could depend on their love and esteem, and their protection, if that ever became necessary. In this case, too, my father had given them a solemn charge to look after me, but he had certainly never anticipated a crisis like this. I was tearing them apart with the conflicts of love and duty.

But I had to go on. I could not turn back, not now.

'Can you guarantee that if you don't shoot me I will not die? It is written in the Quran that once a person is born he has to die. So, go ahead, shoot. I don't mind dying in the name of Christ. In my Bible it is written, "He that believeth in me, though he were dead, yet shall he live" (John 11:25).'

The gun wavered and dropped.

Safdar Shah spoke in the silence. 'You don't want to kill this Christian and get blamed for it. She is already a curse to us. Throw her out.'

They pushed me ahead of them up the stairs. I picked up my bag in the hall and went out of the door. My brothers turned wearily back into the bungalow.

'No weapon that is formed against you shall prosper.' I knew where I had read that (Isaiah 54:17), but I did not know it could be so exactly right.

13: The candle

'Where can I go, Father?' – I stood alone by the side of the Samanabad Road, trying to fight back the tears of shock and pain at the scene I had just experienced, and looking up and down for some clue as to what to do next. But the length of tarmac road was empty of traffic, and the substantial line of bungalows slept behind high walls in the thin morning sunshine, revealing nothing of the prosperous lives going on inside. Almost without thinking I turned to the right and began to walk along the cemented footpath towards the bus stand, a mile away. By the time I reached it I had made up my mind – John and Bimla Emmanuel would give me refuge.

John Emmanuel, a gardener with the city authorities, lived in Medina Colony with his wife and four of their five children. The family attended the Warris Road Church. They had asked me to their house once or twice, and there I had enjoyed myself, talking with them about the Lord and his healing and saving power. They had said, 'Come to us at any time; our home is always open to you.'

At the bus stand there was an assortment of transport. I took a rickshaw to Muzang Chungi, and from there a mini-bus that happened to be going to Gurumangat. From here it was a short walk across the railway line to Medina Colony.

I picked my way along the rutted, dusty path leading between the houses, avoiding the open drains which led to a *houdi* or open cess-tank nearby. At John Emmanuel's house I took the end of the *kunda* hanging outside and banged on the wooden double doors in the high wall. After a slight pause Bimla opened and she stared at me in some surprise, then asked me to enter.

I told her fragments of what had happened and asked for temporary shelter. She saw I was trembling and threw her arms around me: 'You're most welcome to stay with us and whatever we have you can share.'

When John Emmanuel came pedalling home on his bicycle in the later afternoon, he listened to my story with concern. 'Don't worry. I am your brother in Christ,' he assured me. 'How strange that I can feel so at one with people who are not of my kin,' I thought, warmed by his concern. It appeared that the union of true believers with Christ could bind his followers to each other with cords thicker than ties of blood or marriage.

Their house, which they rented, was small – just one living room with a verandah. On one side of this verandah was the kitchen and on the other a toilet. I wondered where we would all sleep – it transpired that I would join the children, the oldest of whom was an eight-year-old girl, on the verandah. This was furnished with blinds, to turn it into a room in colder weather. John and Bimla slept in the compound, as was customary when houses were small and families large. There was no grass nor flowers – there was no room to grow anything. The compound was plastered over with clay and straw to make a hard surface and this was whitewashed, so that it became an extension of the house. There were, however, plants in pots to brighten the place. Simple accommodation compared with the comfort I had left behind me, but it was wonderful to have freedom to take out my Bible and read it openly, and to have times of prayer and study with John and Bimla. I had faced death for this.

That first night, though, lying on the *charpai* under a sheet in the open air, I could not sleep for the unfamiliarity of my surroundings, for my own racing thoughts, and for intrusive night sounds. In that area people went to bed early, so as to be up soon after sunrise to prepare to travel

128

into the city for their work. But as the bustle of daily living was suspended and voices died away from the water pumps, a deep silence fell, into which poured other sounds, noises which demanded that I trace their origins.

There was the squeaking and scuffling of rats. At the back of the houses bad drainage had created puddles of water, in which happy families of frogs noisily disported themselves, and crickets sawed away in the bushes. There was no net to protect me from the whining mosquitos, which danced thick around me. Small rustlings in the straw matting roof of the verandah above made me wonder what lizards or cock-roaches were about to drop onto my head. I envied the children their steady, unconscious sleep. Their gentle breathing grew louder the more I tossed, till it resembled the roaring of a faraway sea.

With an effort I shut my ears and turned my eyes to the strip of sky I could see from under the verandah roof. I tried to send myself to sleep by counting the winking stars, but that only made me more awake. Then the lonely moon rose into my field of vision, bathing the compound in her mysterious light, so beloved of poets and lovers. Then it seemed that some imperious Nawab of a wind, jealous of such silver beauty, summoned torn veils of cloud to screen her face from longing eyes. I watched the dance of the moon and stars across the sky through the changing hours and felt the shocks and sorrows of the day slip into a truer focus.

It was one of those periods of time when the issues of life stand out clearly from the usual muddle in which so much living takes place. I saw that I, Gulshan Esther, poor and hated by those who should care for me, and turned away from their door, was now free of encum-brances. The veil of inherited religion, which had once separated me from a God whom no one could know, had been torn away, revealing Him in the face of Jesus Christ, my Lord. Now the path of discipleship was marked out, and, whether pleasant or painful, I must walk it in obedience. But I was not alone. There was

One with me who was strong and who would provide for all my needs.

Drowsily I saw the paling sky swallow its stars leaving the bright morning star, the herald of the dawn. Thinking of Jesus, the Morning Star of hope, sent by God to light up my life, I fell finally into a short, but untroubled sleep.

I woke up, my eyelids heavy in the full daylight, as the four-year-old boy Gudu tugged at my arm. Even as I struggled to wash with water drawn from the pump in the yard, I thought about the idea which had crystallised overnight – I would need to look for some kind of job since I couldn't expect my friends to keep me.

The Headmistress of the girl's private school looked me up and down as I stood in her office, abashed before this cool and efficient woman, who had about her the air of authority. Yet I was resolute too. She adjusted her shawl and said politely, 'Good morning, madame. How can I help you? Do you have a child here?'

'No, I have no child here. I have come to see if you need a teacher in your school.'

Her expression changed from polite enquiry to one of slight condescension. I could see my direct approach had earned me some black marks. I should have written, not come, like a maid or a gardener, soliciting work.

'What subject do you teach, and what qualifications have you?'

'I can teach Urdu, Islamic Religious Knowledge, history, geography and mathematics, up to matriculation standard.'

She looked at me sharply, as if readjusting her opinions. 'An accomplished teacher of girls,' she said, 'but unfortunately the vacant post that I had is filled, and I can't employ you, but, if you leave your name and address with the secretary, I will get in touch should another vacancy arise.'

She rose from behind a heavy desk to dismiss me, but still I lingered. I was desperate.

'Is it possible that you know of any girls who require

tutoring at home, for any reason, perhaps for illness, or because their parents don't want them to come to school?'

'I regret that I don't. But if I do hear, then I will inform you, if you leave your name and address with the clerk.'

For two or three weeks I had been coming into the city, past the Red Fort, to look for a job, hawking my qualifications around from school to school, like a peddler. The addresses had come from the unemployment office, where I had surprised the clerks by my application. To them I was something of an enigma – a young woman of good caste, with hands that looked unfit for any work, apparently not supported by her family.

John and Bimla assured me again and again of their support, but I knew I was another mouth to feed on one person's low salary. So I prayed for a job and I walked the streets in the baking sun, with a hole in my shoe, and when I felt angry and discouraged I thought about Jesus and how he walked through streets to die on the cross for me.

When I visited the unemployment office for the fourth time I heard that a lady reporter was required for a weekly magazine with offices in Old Anarkali bazaar. I knew the name of Anarkali, the pomegranate flower, as one of these tragic heroines which abound in our history. She was bricked up alive by a moghul emperor, because, through no fault of her own, she fell in love with her own half-brother Saleem. 'Another poor girl in trouble,' I thought, and tried to remember if he bore anything like her awful punishment. Probably not, since he was the emperor's son.

I had seen the magazine, knew that it had 24 pages, with pictures of famous people on the coloured cover, and that it had a political bent. Desperation made me brave, and I asked for an interview there.

At 10 am next day I presented myself at the magazine's first floor offices in Old Anarkali. The editor was a tall, good-looking man, of a fair complexion, who wore a lightweight black suit, and a very pleasant manner indeed.

'Please sit down,' he said, indicating a precisely placed chair a little way away from his polished desk, on the square of carpet. He pressed a buzzer and asked the young man who appeared to fetch me a cold coke. It came in a bottle with a straw.

'I am interested to know why you need a job at all,' he said, and his white teeth showed in a smile.

I said, 'I have no parents and I am educated. I want to earn my living.'

He toyed with a gold-topped pen, and I noticed a faint aroma of perfume, probably from his after-shave. 'But tell me,' he said, 'why do your brothers and sisters not look after you, so that you don't have to work?'

'Oh, they are all married and settled in their own homes and I don't want to be a burden to them, and that is why I need a job.'

He wanted to know where else I had looked for work and I told him of my unsuccessful teaching applications. The light from the net-curtained glazed window fell on my face as we talked and I saw that he was studying me, curiously. Then he appeared to make up his mind about me, remarkably quickly I thought afterwards.

'You can start from tomorrow. Come between 8.30 and 9 o'clock and don't worry – I will tell you certain stock questions which you will ask when interviewing. You will have to work quite hard and go to people's homes – or sometimes to schools.'

'I'm quite experienced at going into people's homes,' I thought but did not say.

He explained that I would be paid a basic salary of 100 rupees a month. This would be set against anything that I earned from the money the ladies paid for the privilege of being interviewed. The idea was that if they paid, they could say what they wanted to say. I would get twenty per cent of that sum. It was a system that worked more to their advantage than mine, but I had no bargaining power.

'You're not a Muslim,' he said. It was more of a statement of fact than a question.

'I am a Christian,' I replied, and waited a long, agonising moment while he pondered. Finally he put the pen back in the top pocket of his jacket, rose from his chair and said, 'Well, it does not matter so much. You seem as you say, an educated person, and not afraid of talking to people.'

He took me out to the editorial office, where I met three male reporters, a photographer, and a calligrapher. He gave me a desk of my own. There was a third room where we ate lunch – provided free. Here worked a *chaprasi*, or peon, who did a number of odd jobs, saw to the post, ran errands, fetched the lunches and made tea.

Next day I arrived for work at the appointed hour and faced my colleagues. I was the only lady among seven men, but if I worried in advance on this score my fears were groundless – they all treated me with great respect, and in the reporters' room I was called 'Baji' (sister). I learned all I could in the next four days, including the ten stock questions. I was determined to succeed.

News, I soon discovered, was written in the editorial room and checked by the editor before being handed to the calligrapher scribing in columns of Urdu script on large sheets of paper. The editor then examined the work to make sure there were no errors before it was taken to the press.

One of my tasks would be to help the editor check the calligrapher's work before sending it to press. Sometimes I had to accompany the *chaprasi* to the post office to take or collect packages.

When the parcels of newly printed magazines returned, it became my work to fold and address them. I became acquainted with labels and gum and enjoyed learning these new tasks while I waited with some trepidation for my first interview. It was to be with the wife of the ex-foreign minister, who had resigned from the government because of personal difficulties with Mr Bhutto, the prime minister. This meant that I would have to put questions which the lady might consider a little intrusive – but I was assured by the editor that she would probably enjoy the chance to put her side of the situation. He was correct, as usual.

I was received by the lady graciously, in her personal sitting room, and asked to sit down. My mind flicked back to that other gracious lady who had ended by putting me in prison. I must confess it gave me some satisfaction now to be a member of the press, and thus the possessor of a little more power than in the past. I was now the inquisitor.

I asked my ten questions, one by one. 'Why has your husband resigned?' 'Are you happy about it?' 'Where were you educated?' and so on.

My questions were not very penetrating, but the fact they were being asked at all of one woman by another and the result was going to be read by thousands of people up and down the country spoke volumes about the changes taking place in society at that time.

Altaf, the photographer, accompanied me on this interview and others. I was thus assured of protection and he was extremely pleased to meet women. One half of his society was still hidden from view and treated like the personal property of the other half. Any modern ideas that were creeping in had a long way to go to balance out against tradition, which still kept men and women in a tight grip, both the rich and educated, as well as the poor and ignorant.

Altaf was useful in other ways, too. The lady let drop, casually, some English words, as she described her life. This embarrassed me very much, because my father's old prohibition had kept this language from me, and now, in a society where it was a hallmark of the right kind of breeding and education, I needed it. But my companion quietly interpreted for me. He also thought of other questions to ask, when my mind went blank.

When all the questions were over, the lady asked me about myself:

'How educated are you?'

'Just enough to interview you,' I told her. She laughed.

'It's not often that one meets a really well educated woman,' she said.

My article, when it appeared, duly rewritten by the editor, had my name, Gulshan, under its title. He would not add the Christian name Esther. The lady paid 700 rupees for it and I got 140 of them. I handed over 100 to John Emmanuel and kept the 40. At first my host and hostess did not want to take my money but I insisted.

'We're very happy that God is helping you,' they said. Well, I was happy too. For the very first time in my life I was succeeding in earning real money, and making my own way by using the education I had received. Imperceptibly, the angry vision of my brothers' faces began to fade into the background.

On another occasion I interviewed the headmistress of the Girls' High School in Lahore. I was nervous about going there, as I felt afraid of tripping up in my questions before a clever woman, enveloped in authority, like a *burka*. But the photographer, Altaf, reassured me:

'Tell her that you want her to explain everything so that the readers will understand. Then listen carefully and write it all down. Don't be afraid to ask simple questions – many of your readers will not want you to be too clever.'

It was good advice. I sat there in all my simplicity, and took a lesson from the headmistress about the difference between a school in private hands and a school that was nationalised. One distinct advantage from the headmistress's point of view seemed to be that she had a freer hand – under the previous owners she had been bossed about a great deal, and the fees kept going up. One disadvantage now was that there were fewer facilities. In addition to this information I noted some details about the room, about the lady herself, about her staff, whom I met too, about the condition of the school, which we were shown around, and about the appearance of the girls.

The photographer enjoyed this interview a great deal, as he was asked to photograph everything, including the girls. They looked very attractive in the white *shalwar kameeze* with its blue *dupatta* that was their uniform, and, I think, found the whole experience an amusing novelty, since they giggled a lot, covering their mouths with their *dupattas*.

My article earned me a commendation from the editor – 'Not bad,' he said. He was not one to go into raptures. I returned to the school three days after the article appeared to collect the balance of the rupees owing to the paper – the interviewees always paid something in advance. I found that the headmistress was now full of curiosity about me, because she had been told something of my story by one of her staff members, who was a Christian.

'Why did you become a Christian? Let me help you come back to your Muslim faith,' the headmistress said. So, in front of her staff I told her a little about it. 'You have a caring attitude, and a strong faith,' said the head.

My nerves were beginning to vanish as no mishaps occurred over what I wrote. I found the work progressively easier, and was getting more used to seeing my name on the articles. It was a strange feeling to think that all over Pakistan my words were being read – and were possibly feeding the aspirations of young women, showing what one of their number could achieve. And yet I, their example, had thoughts and ambitions that lay in a completely different direction, to serve God and do His will. So why was I here, working on this magazine – something so completely out of character with all that had gone before? My pilgrim path had led me here, but for what reason? It was a conundrum, and I usually gave up puzzling on it and just lived from day to day in the two very separate halves of my life, the outer and the inner, the life of work and the life of prayer.

But my fellow-journalists were conscious that I was different from them. After about two weeks they got to know that I was a Christian, though they did not know that I had once been a Muslim too. They teased me about my faith – 'You believe in three Gods,' they said, laughing. I would try to tell them that no, there was only one God, with three manifestations – the Father, Jesus Christ the Son of God, and not just a prophet, and the Holy Spirit, sent at Pentecost to indwell the believers with Christ's own life, teaching and making them holy. But they had been brainwashed since childhood to think of Christianity as inferior to the purity of their monotheistic religion, so how could I change their minds? I noticed however that no one in that office kept the midday prayer time, and I wondered how much their faith meant to them.

The partitions between the offices were made of hardboard and the editor used to put an end to the teasing by coming in and telling the men off. 'Don't tease her. She is the only woman, and you must not be rude to her.'

One day I was going down the steps at 4 pm on my way home when the owner of a sweet shop next door to the paper, Mr Yousef, called to me.

'*A salaam a laikum* (peace be upon you),' he said. I stopped and waited till he came up to me. '*Wah laikum salaam* (the same to you),' I replied.

He said, 'Madame, I have seen you passing by and I think you must be an educated person to work at the magazine. I am looking for a teacher for my three children, and I wonder if you would be interested to take them in the afternoons after your work? We can come to some arrangement about the cost of the lessons.'

I hesitated. The pay from the magazine was not magnificent, as I only went out once or twice a month, unlike the men who went out all the time, even outside Lahore. I went with him into the house and met his wife and children and we all took a liking to each other on the spot and we struck up a bargain then and there. I would teach Urdu, maths, Islamic studies, history and geography to the children when they came from school for two hours a day, from 4 pm to 6 pm. For this I asked for 150 rupees a month and an evening meal each day. I would not come on Sunday.

This new arrangement had one effect. I had to leave my kind friends at Medina Colony, as it would be dark before I got home, and it was not really safe for a woman to walk the streets alone after dark. Lahore had its full complement of pickpockets and kidnappers – I was very familiar now with that side of life since my prison experience. So I took up residence with Mr and Mrs Neelam. They lived on Warris road, near to the church and not too far from Old Anarkali. I knew Mr Neelam from days at Sunrise, when he had been a music teacher.

By December I had written eight or nine stories, all from 'Gulshan' or sometimes 'our lady reporter,' and I felt the editor was pleased with me. In the second week of the month he called me into his office.

'You're doing better than I thought you would,' he said. 'I would like to keep you on here, but one thing is necessary if I do – you must return to the Muslim faith.'

I sat as if turned to stone. He went on:

'Now I know your story, why you are a Christian. But let me tell you, that if your brothers are not helping you I will help you – only give up Christianity. No, listen, I will let you stay at my house. I'll put you in charge of the reporters. I'll get another lady reporter and I'll give you a flat rate salary of 1,000 rupees a month . . .'

With a sickening rush of reality I woke up to the meaning of this speech. This man was in touch with Alim Shah – they were probably friends, going to the same club. He must have known about me all along, and he had been working patiently towards this moment. It was the same old story. 'Show her how much love we Muslims have for each other, then perhaps she'll come back, since she is in need, earning her living and lodging with other people.' And I, who was so pleased with my own writing progress, had failed to wonder just why this man of the world should have taken on and kept on someone as inexperienced as I? But when would they ever learn that I would never return to the fold?

I sighed. 'Don't think I don't appreciate your offer. I should like very much to continue here working for you, but I must tell you that I can't give up being a Christian. Jesus is my life. What I have found in him no other religion can provide.'

Later that day the editor's wife came in to see me, on her way to shop at Old Anarkali – to make one last attempt to get me to change my mind, I supposed.

She called me in to her husband's office while he was busy reading proofs in the reporters' room.

'You're quite clever,' she said. 'Why are you a Christian?'

The implication of her remark made me groan inwardly. To the Muslim all Christians were stupid people, believing a lie. I knew this woman would have no spiritual insight, and I did not feel like going through it all again.

I said gently, 'You will not be able to understand the stage at which I am now. God is so real to me.'

She looked at me and her face hardened. She left without another word.

At the end of the day the editor handed me an envelope with 125 rupees in it. 'I'm sorry,' he said, 'But you can't work here any more. My wife and I will regret your going. We will always remember you.'

'I'm sorry too, but God will find me another job,' I said, with chin held high, but feeling far from brave inside. The editor was obviously struggling with his own humanitarian feelings because he said, as I walked to the door:

'If you're destitute I will help you, but this problem of religion will remain.'

'Don't worry,' I said. 'My God will help me. Before I seek the help of man I will seek the help of God.' And I left his office.

The other reporters were unhappy at seeing me go. 'You've spent so much time with us, and now you're going, just for the sake of a bit of religion. OK, Christ has healed you – why don't you just give some money and leave it at that?'

'He is more to me than that,' I said, and I shook hands with them, and told them I would pray for them. Then I left and walked down the stairs feeling chilled and with my head spinning from the shock of eviction, just when I had begun to feel secure from this particular kind of attack.

Outside I leaned against the wall to steady myself. There must be a reason for all these unsettling experiences. In my heart I cried to my Father in heaven, and He answered swiftly, with a comforting word:

'As thy days, so shall thy strength be. Have not I commanded thee?' I was not aware that just ahead lay my own particular Promised Land, and that I was being prepared to enter in.

14: The witness

'There is a visitor here for you,' said Mrs Neelam on the morning of December 30, and I looked up in surprise from my book.

It was Mr Gill, an elder from the church at Foreman Christian College, who had brought me an invitation. He came straight to the point.

'The Reverend Arthur of the Methodist Church, Foreman Christian College, would like to invite you to preach at his New Year's Day service. You can preach whatever message you are given. What do you say?'

I did not answer for a moment. Foreman Christian College was a big place and the church was bound to be full of influential people. How could I stand up in front of such a crowd and preach? I almost felt like refusing, then I remembered something said to me by God in the night:

'Go and preach among my people.'

When I was healed Jesus had given me a commission to do just that, but then I was not ready. But that glowing vision had illuminated my hard road, teaching me to know God through His Word, and by faith. Was this invitation, coming unsought, the sign that I was ready to tell the Church what I had seen of his great grace and loving kindness?

By now I knew that if a course of action was right several factors would fit together – a way would open, a word would be given, and there would be an inward peace and assurance that the action was right.

I looked up at the messenger. 'I will come,' I said. 'But how will I get there from this house?'

'You will be most welcome to come and stay with my wife and myself tomorrow night at our house in Wadat

Colony. That is near the college, and then we will take you to the service on New Year's Day.'

Kamla Neelam agreed with this idea, and it was arranged that Mr Gill would come for me the next day to conduct me to his house. I went to try and collect my thoughts for the coming test.

The next night, in Mrs Gill's guest room, fear gripped me, as I contemplated what I was about to do. Pride was rearing its head. . . . I did so want to make a good impression.

On my knees I finally uttered the thought aloud: 'How am I going to speak about you? It is nearly four years since I have seen you. How am I going to describe you?'

Put like that it sounded very silly. What did I want? A repeat performance of a sacred experience? As soon as I voiced the thought I realised how ridiculous it was to worry about such things. In the silence of my mind, bowed in God's presence, I heard the still, small voice: 'My spirit will be with you.' Joy flooded in. The promise was enough.

It was undoubtedly the first time in my life I had ever had to face such a crowd. Teachers, professors, nurses, doctors from the nearby Christian hospital – all so well educated, so sure of themselves. Yet I felt an uplifting power come upon me when I witnessed to my healing and told of God's grace to me through so much sorrow. The audience was utterly silent, drinking in every word, never taking their eyes off my face.

As I came down from the pulpit afterwards people came up to me and said what it had meant to them. 'That was with power,' said one or two. 'We didn't even realise the passing of time,' some said, with tears in their eyes. Women going out said, 'You have suffered a lot alone. Let us now share this with you,' and they gave me their addresses.

I was given some of the offering and taken back to Mr Gill's house to have lunch. Through a haze of amazement I thought of my brothers – how I would have loved them to hear about this new turn in the affairs of the sister they had condemned.

As a result of that morning I was invited to take the women's meetings regularly in the church at Foreman Christian College. This meant that I could give up my teaching at Mr Yousef's house, and launch out into the work I really wanted to do – evangelism. All the churches in the area began one by one to invite me to preach, paying my expenses.

During April and May I lived with some friends at Canal Park. In June another family took me into their home and I was there until the day of my sister's son's wedding.

There was to be a women's summer camp at Murree. This area, 8000 feet above sea level, in the foothills of the Himalayas and two and a half hours by bus from Rawalpindi, was an old hill station, dating from the days of the British Raj. Now wealthy people went there for holidays, to enjoy the cooler climate, and the sight of the mountains, with one or two peaks snow-topped for much of the year.

At Murree there was a great deal of Christian activity – a language school for missionaries, a Christian school for missionaries' and other people's children. This, unlike all the schools at sea level, remained open in the summer, and closed for a month in the winter, when deep snow clogged the dangerous mountain roads. Murree was very busy in the summer also with camps and conferences run by Christian groups from all over Pakistan.

The women's camp, at Mubarik, to which I had been invited as main speaker, was for one week, early in June. I was to go on the train to Rawalpindi with the camp leader, Mrs Hadayat, and we were due to leave at 4 o'clock on Friday morning. I was looking forward to the very first train ride of my life.

But on Thursday morning, at around 10 o'clock I received a message from my sister, Samina, who was in Samanabad, preparing for a wedding. Her son was to be married there on Saturday, and she wanted me to be one of the guests.

Her son delivered the invitation verbally in the drawing room of the house where I was a guest. I smiled up at him fondly. From the little I had seen of him during his growing-up years Mahmood was a credit to the family, and I would love to have attended his wedding, but there were great obstacles.

I sent back a verbal reply by Mahmood.

'Please tell your mother that I love her and you dearly, but I cannot come. Everybody will be against me for my beliefs, and my presence will only upset the atmosphere of what should be a happy day for you all. It would not be good form for me to come, and anyway I am going away on Friday to a conference in the hills. I ask you all to accept my apologies at refusing your kind invitation.'

My nephew rode away on his Yamaha, looking glum. I went on with my preparations. By 2 pm Mahmood was back.

'Auntie, you must come to the wedding. My mother says she will not let me be married if you are not there. And I want you to come as well.' And the great big lad had tears in his eyes.

I made a lightning decision. 'The only thing I can say is that I will go to Mr and Mrs Hadayat and ask for their opinion. It is just possible that I could attend your wedding and then leave in time to catch the bus to Rawalpindi, which will link up with one going to Murree on Sunday morning.'

Mahmood's face brightened. 'Can you ride pillion, Auntie? I will take you to Mr and Mrs Hadayat,' he said. So in a short time the neighbours were treated to the spectacle of a young woman roaring off on the back of a motorcycle, clutching tightly at the shirt of the young man in front of her.

When I told my friends the Hadayats about my dilemma, they resolved it instantly, advising me to accept the invitation:

'It will be a witness,' they said. 'Some of your relatives haven't seen you since you were healed.'

That was true. I thought back to that terrible meeting with those uncles. I remembered their hard eyes, popping out of their enraged faces at this cheeky young damsel, daring to defy family custom and Islamic law. It had all happened to a different person. But were they different? I doubted that they would be. Still, there might be one or two chances of witness, and I loved my sister and her son. For their sake I would go.

'You are right,' I said. And once that difficulty was disposed of Mr Hadayat looked up bus times in his diary and we discovered that there was a bus leaving Badami Bagh in Lahore at 12 midnight on Saturday, which would get me to Rawalpindi in time to take another bus to Murree, arriving in good time to speak on Sunday afternoon at my first meeting.

My nephew took me home again on his Yamaha, and promised to come for me next day, to take me to the wedding.

So, the next day, I took a small attache case, and was escorted to Samanabad in great style by my dear nephew.

The wedding, as I predicted, was a disaster from start to finish. Some of the older folk took my presence as a direct offence, and turned their backs on me whenever I appeared in their vicinity. Others, in whom the sense of *Jihad* was strong, picked arguments so that I had hardly any opportunity to talk to my sister Samina, or to Anis, whom I had not seen for about a year.

The main thrust of the attack was, 'Why do you believe in Jesus as the Son of God?'

My Bible was in my case, but I did not need to consult it – the words I needed came to my mouth unbidden, and with power. This opportunity, I realised, would probably not be given to me again, so I spoke to everyone who showed the slightest interest. The arguments raged and I seemed to have no time to eat or drink. My chief opponents, my brothers, I did not see. Safdar Shah had stayed at home when he heard I was coming, and Alim Shah remained with the male guests, out of my reach.

Gradually my opponents fell away, one by one, with such remarks as, 'Oh she is mad, leave her alone,' and

'She is no relation of ours; don't speak to her.'

I suddenly noticed the time. It was 11 pm. I heard a voice saying, 'You are going to witness in Murree tomorrow and you are still here.' Slightly panic stricken I hurried to my sister's room and asked if someone could drop me at Badami Bagh. But Samina's car was being used for other guests, Anis was busy with her in-laws, and some of the other visitors refused point blank – I heard one say, 'We don't want to pollute our car. Ask your Jesus to take you.'

Samina came forward and took my hand – 'Gulshan, I am sorry I can't help you. Why don't you stay with us tonight and then tomorrow we can take you to the bus station?'

It would have been sensible, since there was danger in the streets for a woman alone at this time of night. But a sense of urgency possessed me. I had been given my orders, and had to find my way, somehow. Without taking my farewell I slipped quietly out from the lit house, with all its comforts and security, and stood by the roadside. Clouds were veiling the moon, and houses and trees made fugitive shapes in the darkness. Branches of a big mulberry tree rustled over my head. I moved nervously from under its shadow.

'Lord, you have made me holy. Take care of me and help me to reach the bus station in time. I am all in your hands,' I prayed.

When I ended the prayer the tears were falling. The presence of God was all around me in the darkness, and in that circle I felt safe.

Then I heard far away and coming nearer, the soft purring of a motorcycle engine, and almost immediately saw the headlight, weaving light patterns on the black veil of the night, as the machine bounced towards me along the heat-folded tarmac. I saw it was a hooded rickshaw. Was it bringing a latecomer to the wedding perhaps, or was it taking its driver home after a day's work? Praying that the man would stop for me I waved and the rickshaw drew up at my side.

'Can you get me to Badami Bagh as quickly as you can? I have to catch a bus that leaves for Rawalpindi as soon as possible.'

I could not see his face, since he had on some kind of hood, but he nodded, and in I got, not allowing myself to wonder if he were a villain, who would take advantage of my situation. Off we went, waking the echoes. How quickly we seemed to pass through those streets. When we swung into Badami Bagh it appeared, by my watch, that we had covered the fifteen miles in five minutes. The rickshaw man, without a word, picked up my case and carried it to the Watan Transport bus line, for Rawalpindi. As he swung along in front of me, well built, and dressed in a strange long robe, coloured in a kind of dull brown, I felt he must be a Pathan.

He put my luggage under a seat near the front, and was about to walk away, not waiting for payment, when I stopped him to ask, 'How much do I pay you?'

At this he half turned to me and said, 'God has sent me to help you. Go in peace.' Then he turned back the sleeve of his robe and on his sinewy arm I saw a word written in shiny letters, Patrus (Peter). I tried to see his face but saw only his brilliant eyes.

Tears came to my eyes and I had to wipe them away. When I looked again he had vanished not taking any money. Wondering if I had dreamed the episode, I looked around the bus station, busy at this time of night, when people travelled in preference to the day's heat, but saw only bus passengers stretching their legs in anticipation of a long journey.

I took my place on the cushioned seat, the only lady on the bus travelling alone, and not wearing a *burka*, and I paid the conductor when he asked for the fare.

We stopped for half an hour's refreshment at Jhelum, the half way mark, and again, briefly at Gujarkhan. It grew colder as we ascended into the foothills of the Himalayas. By the time we reached Rawalpindi at about 4.45 am, and forced our way through a throng of people, skinny cows and goats, cars, rickshaws, trucks, bicycles and carts to a bus stand at Raja Bazaar, the sun had started to paint the eastern sky with beaten gold dawn rays.

The bus to Murree was smaller, and the journey was slow and dangerous on a twisting mountain road, with just enough room for two vehicles to pass. It was a much-used road at this time of the year, when the plains baked in the quivering heat. We sat sideways, and I had my back to the mountain wall, so that I did not have to look over the edge at the dangerous slope.

At 11 am we approached Murree. I got off at the post office bus stop, on the slope below the town. I gave my case to a coolie and he led me on a short walk to Mubarik camp. Near the camp the *chowkedar* saw us coming and came to greet me and take the case.

That ladies' camp turned out to be an extraordinary week for me. There were thirty women there from Peshawar, Sialkot, Karachi, Faisalabad (formerly called Lyallpur) and Hyderabad. God put his healing hand on places in lives where women were hurting.

I slept in a two storey building, sharing a room with Ruth, from Abbotabad. There were morning and evening sessions, and mealtimes, with the rest of the day free, but I was very busy a lot of the time talking to women about their burdens. One teacher in a government school in Lahore told me she was having difficulty in witnessing among the Muslims there. We prayed together and talked about the fear that can bind one in such a situation, and I gave her Christ's promise, 'I will not leave you nor forsake you.' She said with joy when we parted, 'You have given me new hope to face all kinds of problems.'

When the women went a group of young people came from Peshawar and the Rev Sayed, who was running the camp site, asked me to stay on to speak to them. One young solicitor came and told me that he was working among Muslims and was ashamed to witness. I told him about Matthew 10:31-33 and prayed with him. On the fourth day he came back and said he had the courage now.

'My fear is over.' It was too. He visited me when I left the camp and went to stay in Rawalpindi with Brother and Sister Younis.

Sister Younis had been at Mubarik and we had formed a bond of fellowship. 'Come and stay with us when you leave here,' she said to me. And so I did.

From those camps my ministry really began in earnest, and I began to go about speaking at conferences, about the way God had dealt with me. I was invited back to Mubarik, that first year, early in July, where I found myself sharing a local convention platform with well-known men in the Christian community. They accepted me as one to whom God had given a ministry. Every time I spoke the invitations came flooding in from places far and near. People wanted to hear what I had to say – they told me that it encouraged them and that it was a message needed for the times.

Opportunities were now about to open up for a larger ministry, but I kept a tight hold on Jesus, at the same time. I knew from experience that when there was blessing there was bound to be attack also. Even so, I was not prepared for the direction from which it came.

15: Conclusion

From Rawalpindi I travelled all over Pakistan, speaking at churches and conferences, and also dealing personally with people in need, both physically and spiritually.

In October 1977 I went to Lahore in answer to a plea from a brother and sister in the Methodist church in Canal Park who wrote that their son was sick. 'Please come and pray for him,' wrote Brother James. I went, praying on the journey.

When I got there the son had been brought home from the United Christian Hospital, on the mend but still weak. Brother and Sister James then asked me to stay with them. They had five daughters as well as five sons and they wanted my help with their upbringing in the things of the Lord. It was agreed in the end that I would stay with them, but be free to go about Pakistan for meetings when needed.

During all these years I was living by faith, the Lord supplying my need, so much so that others wondered if I had some foreign mission backing me. I would try to explain to them that the riches of heaven are at our disposal when we are willing to trust God wholly. I had given God everything – family, house, lands, money, reputation – and was trusting for my needs.

While I was still in Rawalpindi, the final act of Anis Bibi's life on earth was played out. My sister, forced by family opposition to remain a secret believer, died on March 14, 1977. I was with her when she died, comforting her. I know that she put her hand into the hand of the man with the crown, at the top of the ladder, and allowed him to lead her into God's presence.

Anis Bibi's two daughters of 15 and 16 went to live with an uncle after this, since their father appeared not to want to keep them. A few months later I had a message from the girls, asking me if they could come and live with me, since they were not happy. So, in October, I took over the guardianship of my two nieces, and they moved in with me to Brother James's house. There were far too many girls under one roof, and it was then that I really began to pray for a house where I could live my own life, and not be beholden to anyone, except God.

I put the two girls into a convent school, since there were difficulties in leaving my two nieces in someone else's house while I was travelling. The school was run by some kindly sisters, and the atmosphere was good for the girls.

God laid it on the hearts of friends in Karachi to do something about my homeless state. They felt that it was time I had my own house and not have to live all the time with other people, so they raised some money which, added to a little I had already saved, was enough for a small house. What comfort to be able to return to one's very own place after an exhausting series of gospel meetings away somewhere!

When I took over my own house in the summer of 1978 my nieces came to live with me. But all did not go well. I was arraigned before the court on some false accusations.

I told the magistrate that I had been a cripple and been healed by Jesus. He asked if someone from my own family could testify to this. In the interests of justice a member of my family did go into court and attest the story of my healing and speak for my good character. The case against me was dismissed.

My nieces had left me but God was good to me in giving me two lovely adopted daughters, a son and their grandfather as well, so that I would not be alone in the world.

Two months after this in July 1981, I was in Karachi, staying with a friend in Akhtar Colony, near the Methodist church, when I was asked by a young nurse, Patricia, to visit her sister Freda, a nurse in Jinnah Hospital, who, she feared, was possessed by an evil spirit. She said:

'My sister is sick. She cries out, and when the spirit comes she starts screaming and hits out at people.'

I agreed to go with her and we took a rickshaw to the hospital. It was a very hot afternoon, with high humidity, because of the proximity of the ocean. In the young nurse's room at the hospital the atmosphere was clammy and oppressive – but that was not only because of the heat. Freda stood there, young, shy, her head down. She wore her off-duty *shalwar kameeze* and *dupatta*. Now and again she lifted her eyes to look at me with a fixed stare in which there was no expression.

Patricia spoke gently to her sister: '*Ba-ji*, this is Sister Gulshan. She has come to pray for you.'

There was no reply from the young nurse. She stood motionless for a while, then suddenly made an excuse and left the room to go to the bathroom down the hall. After she had been away for fifteen minutes my friend said: 'She is away a long time. I will go and get her.'

She returned, dragging the unwilling younger girl by the arm. Freda sat down on a piece of carpet, and I, seated in an armchair, drew her to sit beside me on the floor. Then I put my hand on her head, and opened my Bible at Psalm 91, and read aloud from it:

'He that dwelleth in the secret place of the Most High shall abide under the shadow of the Almighty.

'I will say of the Lord, he is my refuge and my fortress, my God: in him will I trust.

'Surely he shall deliver thee from the snare of the fowler, and from the noisome pestilence.

'He shall cover thee with his feathers, and under his wings shalt thou trust: his truth shall be thy shield and buckler.'

At this the girl closed her eyes. Still keeping my hand on her head I said: 'I command you in the name of the Lord Jesus to get out of her.'

At this the girl started to rock her body violently, screaming the while, 'Let me go. I am burning.'

I said, 'It is better for you to be burned than for the devil to burn you.'

152

Then the devil spoke, and the voice was different to the girl's own light voice:

'I am going to leave. Please let me go. I will not come back.'

The girl fell down on the floor as the demon left her, and she lay there still, her body relaxed. After ten minutes Patricia helped her to get up. She opened her eyes and asked for water. When she had drunk it I asked her to come and sit beside me again. This time she rested her head on my knee and said, 'Please pray more for me. I feel much lighter.'

I asked her to repeat this prayer, 'Thank God that I have been freed and now I commit my life to you. Take it and use me for your purpose, and give me strength to follow you and remain faithful.'

We sat until 7 pm when more nurses came into the room. They learned what had happened, and they started to bring their problems, asking me to pray for them. One had an examination she feared. Another had headaches on the ward. A third had parents at home sick. And so I did pray for them.

I omitted to say that all this long afternoon and evening we had lunch and tea in that room. It was such a vivid day, and every memory seemed heightened – even the taste of the turnips, beef chops, chapattis and banana that we ate.

When it was time to leave, Patricia and I took a rickshaw back to Akhtar Colony, where I was staying with another friend. I have a lovely picture of those two sisters to remind me. They are really beautiful girls, and they witness now for Jesus in the hospital.

The Lord has used me in healing situations where people had quarrels with one another. I suppose I have been misunderstood so much myself that I know what a fire can be started with one unkind word, one malicious thought.

Because I have no church backing we have to look to the Lord direct to supply all our needs. Sometimes we wake up in the morning and there is no food at all in the house. We wait then to see how the need will be met. But there are days when we all decide, partly from necessity, that it will be a fast day. On these occasions we draw near to God. He is our Father. He knows what is best and He does not fail us, only tests us for a season.

In my poverty, the poor are drawn to me. People come, walking for miles, without the bus fare to go home – and we find ourselves giving from our meagre store. They come for spiritual help, but how can we let them go, without meeting their physical needs as well? 'Freely ye have received, freely give.'

I was called to the bedside of a man who had come from England, who was suffering from ameobic dysentery and a cyst. This was in January 1981. I prayed for him and laid hands on him and he recovered. The result of this was that I ended up in England, and Canada, preaching to groups of Asian and English people.

The great fear in my aunt's mind, when I first testified to my healing by Jesus, was that I should go to England. Well, here I am, looking back over all the way that my heavenly Father has led me, since I first trusted him.

I can see that the pilgrimage which my father embarked on with me was the start of my soul's quest to know God. It raised hopes which, though disappointed at Mecca, drove me, especially after my father's death, to seek God in an urgent and desperate way. I stretched out my hand to Jesus the Healer – not knowing anything about him except the little I read in the Quran – and I was made whole.

Today I am a witness to the power of God to reach people who are behind the veil of Islam. That veil can be torn away, so that they can see Jesus, hear him and love him.

Today I no longer need the Five Pillars of Islam to support my faith. My 'Witness' is to Jesus, crucified, dead and buried, then raised in resurrection life, and now living in his own people. My *namaz* is not to an unknowable God but to one whose story is found in his own Word, the Holy Bible, my most precious treasure, which is written on the tablets of my heart and mind, just as the Quran used to be. My *zakat* is no longer a proportion, but the whole of my income, for everything I have belongs to God. My riches are stored up in heaven. My fasting is not done at Ramadan, to placate God, so that I might be sure of Paradise, but it is done with delight, so that I might know Him better. My *Hajj* is my journey through life. Each day brings me nearer my goal – to be with Jesus, my heavenly King, for ever.

The blood of bulls, sheep or goats can never wipe away sin, but we may enter into the holiest place in perfect acceptance, through a new and living way, 'through the veil,' that is to say, his flesh. For this man (Jesus) when he had offered one sacrifice for sin for ever, sat down on the right hand of God (Hebrews 10:12).

Such is Jesus, Lamb of God, prophet and priest, King of Kings, my Lord and my God.